UNLEASH
THE TRADER WITHIN

UNLEASH
THE TRADER WITHIN

KEY TO UNLOCKING YOUR FINANCIAL FREEDOM

TARUN SHARMA

Unleash the Trader Within
Tarun Sharma

Published by White Falcon Publishing

All rights reserved
First Edition, 2023
© Tarun Sharma, 2023
Cover design by White Falcon Publishing, 2023

No part of this publication may be reproduced, or stored in a retrieval system, or transmitted in any form by means of electronic, mechanical, photocopying or otherwise, without prior written permission from the publisher.

The contents of this book have been certified and timestamped on the Gnosis blockchain as a permanent proof of existence. Scan the QR code or visit the URL given on the back cover to verify the blockchain certification for this book.

The views expressed in this work are solely those of the author and do not reflect the views of the publisher, and the publisher hereby disclaims any responsibility for them.

Requests for permission should be addressed to the publisher.

ISBN - 978-1-63640-924-5

"Financial freedom is not merely about accumulating wealth, but the liberation to live life on your own terms, guided by your passions and purpose, unrestricted by financial constraints."
- Tarun Sharma

CONTENTS

Preface & Book Dedication ix

1 What is Financial Freedom 1

2 How to Achieve Financial Freedom 3

3 How the Stock Market Can Help 7
    a. Segments available in Stock Market 10
    b. How to get Started 12
    c. Importance of Learning before you Enter in the market 14

4 The Psychology of a New Trader vs The Psychology of a
    Professional Profitable Trader 17

5 The Impact of Emotions & Risk management 19

6 Technical vs Fundamental Analysis 22

7 Type of Traders 24

8 Why Day Trading can be Your Path to Financial Freedom 28

9 Trading rules for all beginners 31

10 Different stages for traders 36

11 Decoding Price Action:
     The Hidden Language of the Markets 39

12 5 Star Setup 117
   a. Trading Strategies 117
   b. Process for the 5 min breakout strategy: 121

BONUS CONTENT FOR OUR BOOK READERS AND STUDENTS BY TWT..137

13 MSM Concept 138

14 Trader Daily Rituals 147

15 The Power of Trading Psychology 149

16 Daily Affirmation for Traders for a Strong Mindset 169

17 How to Control Overtrading 171

18 TWT 3-3-4 Concept 173

19 Secret Sauce to become an Independent Trader 175

20 Trading Journal Sample 179

21 My Trading Journey 180

22 Letter to the Day Trader from the Author 187

23 Disclaimer for Readers 189

PREFACE

Dear Readers,

I am thrilled to present my book, "Unleash the Trader Within," which delves into the world of price action and technical analysis. As a passionate student of the financial markets, I have always been intrigued by the interplay between market dynamics and human behaviour.

Through years of study and practice, I have come to believe that the key to success in trading lies in understanding these interactions and utilizing technical analysis to make informed decisions.

The goal of this book is to make its learners independent and profitable traders. By offering a comprehensive guide to price action and technical analysis, I aim to equip you with the knowledge and skills necessary to navigate the markets with confidence and achieve financial success.

I am grateful to my mentor, Mr. Tony Robbins, for inspiring and motivating me to pursue my passions and make a difference in the world. His teachings on personal development and mastery have been instrumental in shaping my outlook on life and driving me towards excellence.

Also, I want to thank Mr. Dharam Veer Sood & Arjit Mehrotra for unconsciously encouraging me to write a book.

In this book, I share my knowledge and experience and provide practical tools and insights that will help you develop a deep understanding of price action and technical analysis. Whether you are a seasoned trader or just starting out, I believe that this book will provide valuable guidance that will help you unleash the hidden trader within you.

I hope you find this book informative, engaging, and empowering.

Best regards,

Tarun Sharma

> **PS:**
> **This book is dedicated to my father,**
> **Late. Sh Tej Bhan Sharma, who has been**
> **my direct and indirect strength throughout my life.**

CHAPTER 1
WHAT IS FINANCIAL FREEDOM

Financial freedom is a concept that has the power to completely transform your life. Can you imagine waking up every day without a care in the world when it comes to money? No more worrying about how you'll pay your bills, no more sacrificing your time and energy just to make ends meet. Instead, you have the freedom to follow your dreams, travel to new and exciting places, or simply relax and enjoy life to the fullest.

But what is the secret to achieving financial freedom? It all comes down to passive income streams. By investing your money in assets that generate a steady flow of income, such as stocks, bonds, real estate, or businesses, you can achieve financial independence.

But it's not just about making money. Financial freedom also requires smart financial decision-making and discipline. You must take control of your finances, pay off debt, and invest for the future.

Here's the best part: Financial freedom is achievable for anyone! With the right mindset and the right tools, you too can reach a state of financial independence and live life on your own terms.

Financial freedom is a journey, not a destination. It requires persistence and a lifelong commitment to smart financial decision-making. But with hard work and determination, anyone can achieve financial freedom and enjoy the many benefits that come with it.

So start your journey today. Take control of your finances, invest in your future, and experience the freedom and peace of mind that comes with financial independence.

By reading this book, you have already taken that first step towards it. Congratulations!

CHAPTER 2

HOW TO ACHIEVE FINANCIAL FREEDOM

Let me take this moment to welcome you to the exciting world of financial freedom, where you can achieve financial independence and live life on your own terms. Financial freedom is the ultimate goal for many people, and it's a journey that begins with a simple idea: that you can take control of your finances and create a life of abundance and security.

As you turn the pages of this book, you'll learn the secrets to achieving financial freedom and discover the steps you need to take to turn your dreams into reality. Whether you're just starting out on your financial journey or you're a seasoned investor looking to take your wealth to the next level, this guide is designed to help you achieve your goals and live the life you've always wanted.

So, let's dive in!

Step 1: Know your numbers.

The first step to achieving financial freedom is to understand your current financial situation. This means taking a close look at your income, expenses, debts, and assets. You need to know exactly how much money you're earning, how much you're spending, and how much you owe. Once you have a clear understanding of your financial situation, you can start to make informed decisions about how to achieve your goals.

Step 2: Set your goals

The next step is to set clear, realistic financial goals. This could be paying off debt, building an emergency fund, saving for retirement, or investing in the stock market. Whatever your goals are, make sure they are specific, measurable, achievable, relevant, and time-bound (SMART). This will help you stay focused and motivated as you work towards your financial goals.

Step 3: Create a budget

The third step to achieving financial freedom is to create a budget. A budget is a plan that outlines how you will allocate your money each month to meet your financial goals. It's important to stick to your budget, even when things get tough. A budget helps you stay focused and on track and makes it easier to reach your financial goals.

Step 4: Invest in yourself

The fourth step to achieving financial freedom is to invest in yourself. This means taking the time to learn about personal finance, investing, and wealth building. The more you know, the better equipped you will be to make informed decisions about your money. Read books, attend seminars, and seek advice from experts to help you grow your wealth and achieve your financial goals.

Step 5: Invest in assets

The fifth step to achieving financial freedom is to invest in assets. Assets are things that generate income or appreciate in value over time. Examples of assets include stocks, bonds, real estate, and rental properties. Investing in assets is a key component of building wealth and achieving financial freedom.

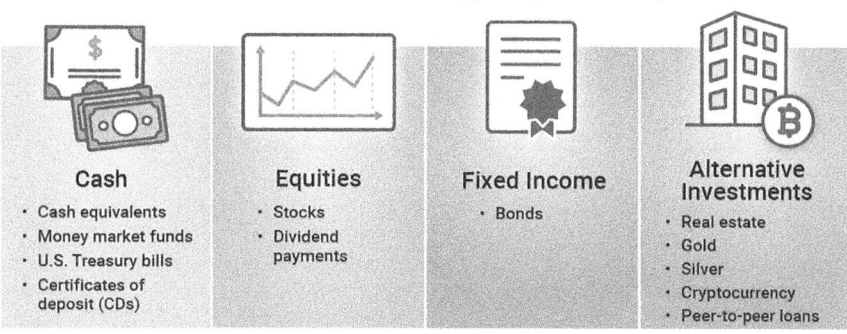

ASSET CLASSES — Diversifying your portfolio by investing in different types of assets can help protect you from volatility.

Cash
- Cash equivalents
- Money market funds
- U.S. Treasury bills
- Certificates of deposit (CDs)

Equities
- Stocks
- Dividend payments

Fixed Income
- Bonds

Alternative Investments
- Real estate
- Gold
- Silver
- Cryptocurrency
- Peer-to-peer loans

Step 6: Be patient and disciplined.

The final step to achieving financial freedom is to be patient and disciplined. Building wealth and achieving financial freedom takes time and hard work. It's important to stay focused, be patient, and stick to your plan. Don't get discouraged by setbacks or unexpected expenses. Stay the course, and you'll eventually reach your financial goals.

So, there you have it, the six steps to achieving financial freedom. Remember, financial freedom is not a destination, but a journey. The more you learn and the more you take action, the closer you will get to achieving your financial goals and living the life you've always wanted.

So, start your journey today, and let's make financial freedom a reality!

CHAPTER 3
HOW THE STOCK MARKET CAN HELP

In our quest for financial freedom, many of us may have heard the term "stock market" thrown around as a potential solution. But what exactly is the stock market, and how can it help us achieve financial freedom?

Picture yourself as the protagonist in an exciting adventure, embarking on a journey towards financial stability and independence. The stock market is like a vast treasure trove, filled with untold riches waiting to be claimed by those who are brave enough to venture forth.

At its core, the stock market is a marketplace where stocks, which are small pieces of ownership in a company, are bought and sold. When you purchase a stock, you become a part-owner of the company and are entitled to a portion of its profits. This can be a lucrative way to grow your wealth over time, as successful companies typically see their stock prices increase.

The key to success in the stock market is to invest in high-quality companies with a proven track record of success. This requires research and due diligence, as well as a healthy dose of patience and discipline. You must be willing to hold onto your stocks for the long term, weathering the ups and downs of the market, in order to see real results.

To maximize your chances of success, it's important to educate yourself about the stock market and learn as much as you can about the companies, you're considering investing in. This could include reading financial reports, analysing market trends, and seeking out expert advice.

So, like the hero in an epic adventure story, arm yourself with knowledge and determination, and set out on the quest for financial freedom through the stock market. With patience and perseverance, you too can reach your destination and secure your financial future.

The stock market has been a popular investment vehicle for many people looking to grow their wealth and attain financial independence. Here's how:

Potential for high returns: Investing in the stock market has the potential to generate high returns over the long term. Historically, stocks have produced an average return of around 10% per year, which can significantly outpace inflation and provide a solid foundation for building wealth.

Diversification: Investing in the stock market allows you to diversify your portfolio and reduce risk. By owning a mix of stocks in different industries and countries, you can spread out your investments and reduce the impact of any single stock's performance on your overall portfolio.

Compound interest: The stock market can also help you take advantage of the power of compound interest. When you invest in stocks, the returns you earn can be reinvested and compounded over time, allowing your wealth to grow even faster.

Long-term investment: Investing in the stock market is a long-term investment, which is ideal for those looking to achieve financial freedom. By holding onto stocks for several years, you can weather any short-term market fluctuations and benefit from the long-term growth potential of the stock market.

Passive income: Another benefit of investing in the stock market is the potential for passive income. By investing in dividend-paying stocks, you can receive a steady stream of income without having to actively manage your investments.

Of course, it is important to remember that investing in the stock market does come with some risks. It is crucial to conduct thorough research and seek out advice from a financial advisor before making any investment decisions. Additionally, having a well-diversified portfolio and a long-term investment horizon can increase your chances of success.

Another crucial aspect of successful stock market investing is patience. The stock market can be volatile in the short term, but over the long term, it has a history of delivering positive returns. By avoiding impulsive reactions and adhering to a long-term investment strategy, you can minimize the impact of short-term market fluctuations on your portfolio.

It's also important to keep in mind the significance of proper asset allocation. This means dividing your investments between different asset classes, such as stocks, bonds, and real estate, to create a well-diversified portfolio. This can help reduce the impact of any single investment's performance on your overall portfolio and improve your chances of success.

Finally, it's a good idea to educate yourself about the stock market and personal finance. Read books, attend workshops, or seek out a financial advisor who can help you create a plan that works for you. The more you know about the stock market and personal finance, the better equipped you'll be to make informed investment decisions and achieve financial freedom.

Investing in the stock market can be a powerful tool in achieving financial freedom. By taking advantage of its potential for high returns, diversification, compound interest, and passive income, you can work towards building a solid financial foundation for the future.

Segments available in Stock Market

As you embark on your journey towards financial freedom through the stock market, you'll discover a fascinating world of different investment options. With so many segments to choose from, it's like being a kid in a candy store! Let's take a closer look at the different segments available in the stock market.

Equity: This segment is where you can invest in individual stocks and become a part-owner of the company. It's a great way to benefit from the long-term success of the company and grow your wealth over time.

Bonds: This segment is for those who prefer a more predictable and steady return on their investment. When you invest in bonds, you are essentially lending money to a company or government, which pays you back with interest over a specified period of time.

Mutual Funds: This segment allows you to invest in a professionally managed portfolio of stocks, bonds, or other securities. It's a great option for those who want to diversify their investments and benefit from the expertise of a professional fund manager.

Exchange-Traded Funds (ETFs): Similar to mutual funds, ETFs allow you to invest in a diverse portfolio of stocks, bonds, or other securities. However, they are traded on the stock exchange like individual stocks and can be bought or sold at any time during the trading day.

Derivatives: This segment includes financial products like options and futures, which are based on the price of an underlying asset, such as a stock or commodity. It is a more advanced form of investing and is generally only recommended for experienced investors.

Currency: This segment includes all currency-related trading, including crypto trading, which is the next big thing in the stock market. Most of the new traders are attracted towards it.

Each segment of the stock market offers its own unique advantages and disadvantages, and the right choice for you will depend on your investment goals, risk tolerance, and overall financial situation. With so many options to choose from, the stock market truly is a place where there's something for everyone!

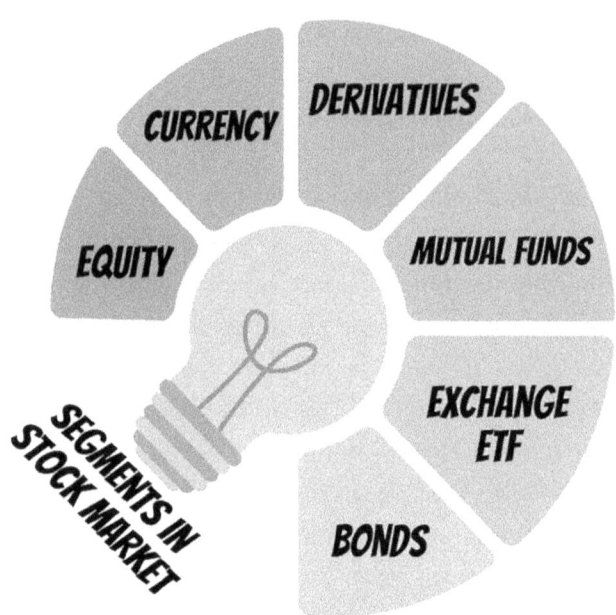

How to get Started

Getting started in the stock market can seem intimidating, but with the right approach, it can be relatively straightforward. Here are the steps to help you get started:

Determine your investment goals: What do you want to achieve with your investments? Are you saving for retirement, building an emergency fund, or trying to generate income? Knowing your investment goals will help guide your investment decisions and ensure that you stay on track.

Assess your risk tolerance: How much risk are you comfortable taking on? This will help you determine which types of investments are right for you and help you create a well-diversified portfolio.

Open a brokerage account: You'll need to open a brokerage account in order to start investing in the stock market. There are many different types of brokerage accounts available, so it's important to choose one that meets your investment goals and risk tolerance.

Educate yourself: It's important to educate yourself about the stock market and personal finance. Read books, attend workshops, or seek out a financial advisor who can help you create a plan that works for you. The more you know, the better equipped you'll be to make informed investment decisions.

Start investing: Once you have opened a brokerage account and educated yourself about the stock market, you can start investing. You can begin with a small amount of money and gradually increase your investments over time as you become more comfortable.

Monitor your investments: Regularly review your investments and make adjustments as needed to ensure that your investments continue to align with your goals. It's also a good idea to seek out professional advice if you have any questions or concerns.

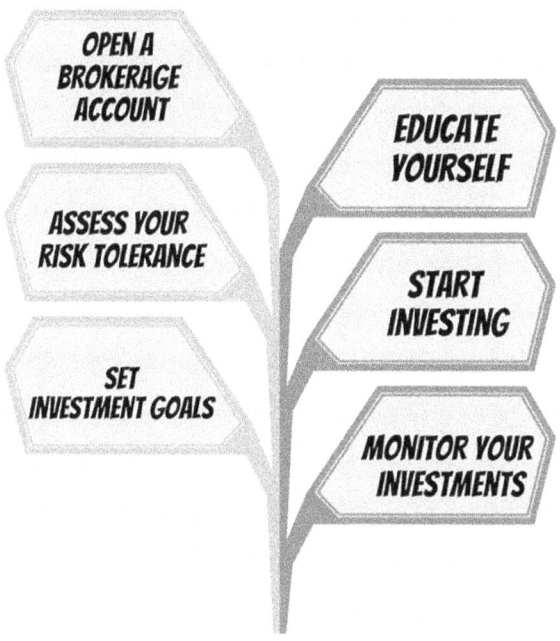

Importance of Learning before you Enter in the market

"Learn before You Earn"

First of all, let's start by understanding that the stock market can be complex, but with the right knowledge and education, it can also be a great way to grow your wealth over time.

One of the key benefits of learning about the stock market is that it can help you make informed investment decisions. By understanding the different types of stocks, how to read financial statements, and how to analyze market trends, you'll be better equipped to identify good investment opportunities and make decisions that are more likely to lead to success.

Another important reason to learn about the stock market is to avoid common mistakes that many investors make. For example, by learning about the importance of diversification and how to avoid overreacting to market volatility, you can minimize the risks associated with investing in the stock market.

It is also crucial to keep up-to-date with the latest developments in the stock market. By continually educating yourself and staying informed, you will be better prepared to make informed investment decisions and adapt to changes in the market.

Finally, learning about the stock market can help you identify opportunities for growth and wealth creation. By understanding the various investment opportunities available, you'll be better positioned to find opportunities that align with your goals and risk tolerance.

Learning is a key aspect of success in the stock market. By continually educating yourself and staying informed, you can increase your chances of achieving financial freedom through investing in the stock market. So, don't be afraid to get started and keep learning!

We all know someone who has been bitten by the stock market bug. Maybe it's a friend, a family member, or even ourselves. The stock market can be an exciting and lucrative place, but it can also be a dangerous one if you don't approach it with the right mindset. That's why I want to share with you the story of my old friend Rahul Malhotra and the lessons he learned about the importance of learning before starting stock market trading.

Rahul has always had a passion for the stock market. He dreamed of achieving financial freedom and the ability to provide for his family in a way that he never could before. However, despite his dreams, Rahul never took the time to truly educate himself about the stock market and how it works.

So, when he finally took the plunge and started trading, he felt like he was on top of the world. He was making trades based on tips and news, and he was sure that he was going to make a fortune. However, as time passed, Rahul realized that he had made some poor investment decisions. The market was volatile, and he was losing money with every trade. He felt defeated and helpless, and he didn't know how to turn his situation around.

That's when Rahul met a successful stock trader who offered to help him. The trader took Rahul under his wing and taught him everything he needed to know about the stock market. He loaned Rahul books, resources, and even taught him how to analyze the market. Rahul was determined to make a change, and he dedicated himself to learning everything he could about the stock market.

Months went by, and Rahul's hard work and dedication paid off. He was now making informed investment decisions and watching his portfolio grow. He felt proud of what he had accomplished and grateful for the person who helped him along the way.

Rahul's story is a testament to the importance of learning and dedication in the stock market. It's a reminder that anything is possible with the right mindset and a willingness to learn. If Rahul had taken the time to educate himself before starting to trade, he could have avoided the initial losses and frustration he experienced. Instead, he had to go through a difficult journey to get to where he wanted to be.

So, to all of you out there who are interested in the stock market, remember Rahul's story and take the time to educate yourselves. The stock market can be a powerful tool for achieving financial freedom, but only if you approach it with the right mindset and dedication. Don't be like Rahul and make costly mistakes. Take the time to learn and understand the market, and you'll be well on your way to financial freedom.

CHAPTER 4
THE PSYCHOLOGY OF A NEW TRADER VS THE PSYCHOLOGY OF A PROFESSIONAL PROFITABLE TRADER

The stock market can be a challenging and unpredictable place, and the way traders approach their investments can have a significant impact on their success. While the psychology of a new trader and a professional profitable trader may seem similar, there are key differences between the two that can impact their investment outcomes. In this blog, we'll compare and contrast the psychology of a new trader and a professional, profitable trader.

The Psychology of a New Trader

New traders often approach the stock market with a mix of excitement and fear. The excitement of potential gains can lead to impulsive and poorly thought-out trades, while the fear of losing money can result in indecision and a failure to take advantage of investment opportunities. New traders may also be overwhelmed by the complex nature of the stock market and lack the knowledge and experience to make informed investment decisions.

The Psychology of a Professional Profitable Trader

In contrast, professional profitable traders approach the stock market with a level of confidence and discipline. They have a solid understanding of the market and are familiar with different investment strategies and techniques. They are able to make informed investment decisions, manage their emotions, and avoid impulsive trades. Professional profitable traders are patient and dedicated, and are focused on their long-term investment goals.

The Importance of Patience and Dedication

One of the key differences between new traders and professional, profitable traders is their approach to patience and dedication. New traders often lack the patience and dedication required to succeed in the stock market, while professional, profitable traders understand the importance of taking the time to research and analyze their investments. This dedication and patience allow them to make sound investment decisions and avoid impulsive trades that can negatively impact their portfolio.

CHAPTER 5

THE IMPACT OF EMOTIONS & RISK MANAGEMENT

The Impact of Emotions

Emotions play a significant role in the psychology of both new traders and professional profitable traders. However, the way in which these emotions are managed can have a significant impact on investment outcomes. New traders are often more susceptible to the influence of their emotions, while professional profitable traders have developed the skills to manage their emotions and avoid impulsive trades.

The psychology of a new trader and a professional profitable trader can have a big impact on their investment outcomes. New traders are often driven by excitement and fear, while professional profitable traders are focused on patience, dedication, and discipline. By taking the time to educate themselves and develop a solid understanding of the stock market, new traders can learn from the psychology of professional profitable traders and increase their chances of success.

Another key difference between new traders and professional, profitable traders is their approach to learning and education. New traders often enter the stock market with limited knowledge and experience, which can make it difficult for them to make informed investment decisions. On the other hand, professional, profitable traders understand the importance of continuing their education and staying up-to-date with market developments. They are dedicated to learning and improving their investment strategies and are always seeking out new opportunities for growth.

One-way new traders can learn from professional profitable traders is by seeking out educational resources such as books, online courses, and seminars. These resources can provide a comprehensive understanding of the stock market and investment strategies and can help new traders develop the knowledge and skills they need to succeed. Additionally, many professional profitable traders are more than willing to share their experiences and insights and can provide valuable guidance and advice to new traders.

The Importance of Risk Management

Risk management is an essential aspect of successful stock market trading, and the way in which new traders and professional, profitable traders approach risk management can have a big impact on their investment outcomes. New traders are often more likely to take on excessive risk, while professional, profitable traders understand the importance of managing risk and avoiding excessive losses.

Professional and profitable traders employ a range of risk management strategies, including diversification, stop-loss orders, and position sizing. These strategies help them minimize their exposure to risk and protect their portfolio from significant losses. By taking a structured and disciplined approach to risk management, professional and profitable traders can preserve their capital and increase their chances of success.

In a nutshell, the psychology of a new trader and a professional, profitable trader can have a big impact on their investment outcomes. New traders can learn from professional, profitable traders by seeking out educational resources, focusing on patience and dedication, and adopting a structured and disciplined approach to risk management. By developing these skills, new traders can increase their chances of success and attain their financial goals.

CHAPTER 6

TECHNICAL VS FUNDAMENTAL ANALYSIS

As you sit back and relax with a cup of tea in hand, ready to delve into the world of stock market trading, I invite you to imagine a scene. You are standing at the crossroads of two paths, one leading to the world of technical analysis and the other to the world of fundamental analysis.

On one hand, you have technical analysis, a method that focuses on the use of charts and technical indicators to analyze past market data and make predictions about future price movements. This approach is favored by traders who believe that market trends, patterns, and signals can be used to gain insight into the future direction of a stock's price.

On the other hand, you have fundamental analysis, a method that looks at a company's financial and economic data to determine its intrinsic value and future growth potential. This approach is favored by traders who believe that a company's underlying financial strength is the best indicator of its future success.

So, which path will you choose? Will you follow the technical analyst, who spends hours poring over charts and indicators, or will you join the fundamental analyst, who delves into balance sheets and income statements in search of hidden value?

The truth is, there is no one-size-fits-all answer to this question. Every trader is unique and has their own individual investment goals and preferences. Some traders prefer the fast-paced, data-driven world of technical analysis, while others prefer the more methodical and data-driven approach of fundamental analysis.

And then, there are those traders who choose to walk down both paths. They believe that the best way to make informed investment decisions is to use a combination of both technical and fundamental analysis. They use technical analysis to identify key support and resistance levels, trend lines, and then use fundamental analysis to validate these signals. This approach allows traders to take advantage of the strengths of both methods and make informed investment decisions based on a more comprehensive understanding of the market.

So, whether you choose to use technical analysis, fundamental analysis, or a combination of the two, remember this: education is key. The more you learn about each approach and its strengths and weaknesses, the better equipped you will be to make informed investment decisions that align with your individual investment goals.

So, let's start our journey into the world of stock market analysis and discover the path that's right for you. Buckle up, and let's go!

CHAPTER 7

TYPE OF TRADERS

The stock market is a vast and complex arena, filled with a diverse cast of characters. From adrenaline-fueled day traders to patient, long-term investors, each player brings their own unique style and strategy to the table. But who are these traders, and how do they approach the market? Let's take a closer look at the different types of traders in the stock market, and the approaches that define each one.

Day Traders: These traders live for the thrill of the moment, darting in and out of positions with lightning speed. They're always on the lookout for short-term market movements and fluctuations, and they're not afraid to take calculated risks to seize the opportunity.

Swing Traders: These traders take a more measured approach, holding onto positions for several days to a few weeks. They're in it for the intermediate-term trends and fluctuations, and they're always searching for the sweet spot where short-term gains meet long-term stability.

Position Traders: These traders are in it for the long haul, holding positions for several months or even years. They take a big-picture view of the market, seeking out the underlying long-term trends and fluctuations that drive the market over time.

Value **Investors**: These traders are always on the hunt for hidden gems, seeking out undervalued stocks with the potential for long-term growth and stability. They believe that a company's true worth is reflected in its earnings and balance sheets, and they're always looking for ways to get in early and reap the rewards.

Growth Investors: These traders are always on the lookout for the next big thing, seeking out high-growth companies that are expected to generate significant earnings and revenue growth in the future. They're willing to take a risk on a company with a proven track record of success, even if the price tag is high.

Momentum Traders: These traders believe that past performance is the best indicator of future success, and they invest in stocks that are showing strong momentum. They pay close attention to factors such as recent price movements, earnings reports, and analyst recommendations, and they are always on the lookout for the next hot stock.

Technical Traders: These traders rely on technical analysis and chart patterns to make their investment decisions, rather than fundamental analysis. They believe that the stock market follows a pattern that can be predicted and capitalized upon, and they use tools like trend lines and support/resistance levels to make their decisions.

Fundamental Traders – Fundamental traders are savvy market participants who make trading decisions based on fundamental analysis. They dive deep into financial statements, economic indicators, and industry trends to uncover the true value of an asset. Unlike short-term traders, they take a long-term view and aim to buy undervalued assets and sell overvalued ones. By doing so, they capitalize on market mispricing and seek substantial gains. Their expertise brings efficiency to market valuations and contributes to the overall dynamics of the financial world.

Each of these types of traders has their own unique approach and strategy, but they all share one thing in common: a deep passion for the stock market and a drive to succeed. Whether you're just starting out or you're a seasoned veteran, the key to success in the stock market is to find the approach that works best for you and to continuously educate yourself and stay informed about the latest trends and developments. So turn the page, and let's delve deeper into the world of stock market trading.

Choosing the right trading style in the stock market can be a bit like discovering your true self. It requires introspection, an understanding of your personality, risk tolerance, and financial goals.

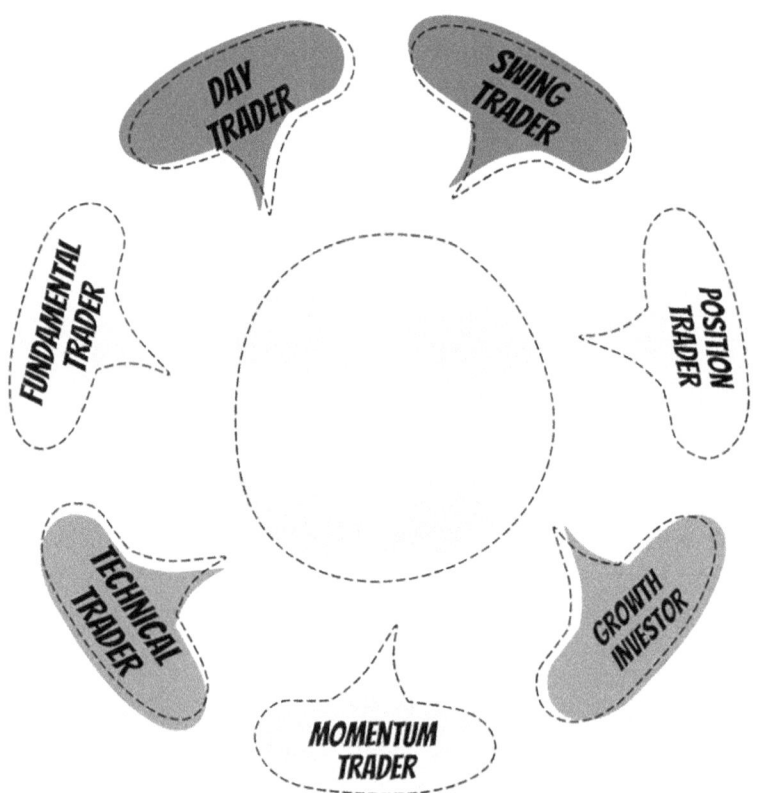

Here is a guide to help you find the perfect fit:

Get to know yourself: Assess your risk tolerance and determine how much uncertainty you can handle. This will help you choose a trading style that aligns with your comfort level.

Dream big: What are your financial goals? Do you want to make quick profits or are you in it for the long haul? Your goals will play a big role in determining your trading style.

Learn about the different styles: There are various trading styles to choose from, such as day trading, swing trading, and long-term investing. Take the time to understand each one and see which one speaks to you.

By following these steps, you'll be on your way to finding the trading style that will lead you to financial freedom.

CHAPTER 8

WHY DAY TRADING CAN BE YOUR PATH TO FINANCIAL FREEDOM

In the world of day trading, the markets are a living, breathing entity, pulsing with vibrant energy that sets the heart racing. They are a place of endless possibilities, where fortunes are made and dreams are realized, and where the call of the markets is felt in every beat of the heart.

To be a day trader is to be part of a living, breathing organism. It is to be immersed in a world of constant motion, where every second counts and every decision can mean the difference between success and failure. It is a place where the thrill of the chase is matched only by the rush of a successful trade, where the highs are sky-high, and the lows are crushing.

But it is not just the excitement that draws people to the markets. It is the promise of something more, something greater than oneself. Day trading is a path that offers the chance to be one's own boss, to set one's own schedule, to work from anywhere in the world. It is a path to freedom, a way to escape the confines of a traditional career and to live life on one's own terms.

And then there is the wealth. The chance to earn a fortune, to make more money in a single day than most people make in a year. It is the allure of riches, the promise of a life beyond one's wildest dreams.

I want to share my friend's journey with you. Five years ago, he was stuck in a job that he didn't enjoy and barely made enough money to pay his bills. He knew he needed a way out, but he didn't know what to do.

One day, a friend introduced him to the world of day trading. At first, he was skeptical - he had heard stories of people losing everything in the stock market. But as he learned more about day trading, he realized that it was a way to take control of his financial future.

He started small, investing just a few thousand rupees that he had saved up. At first, he made some mistakes - he bought and sold on impulse, without really understanding the market. But as he gained experience, he began to see patterns and trends that allowed him to make better trades.

Over time, his profits grew. He reinvested his earnings back into the market and soon, he was making more money trading than he was at his day job. He quit his job and became a full-time day trader, focusing on the stock market and foreign exchange.

Day trading allowed him to achieve financial freedom. He was able to buy a house, take vacations, and save for his future. He didn't have to worry about living paycheck to paycheck anymore. Instead, he had control over his financial destiny.

For those who are willing to put in the time and effort, who are willing to embrace the excitement and face the risks head-on, day trading can be an incredibly rewarding path. It is a journey that will challenge the mind, excite the soul, and reward the brave.

So if you feel the call of the markets, if you feel the pull of the heartbeat of the market, then heed the call and embark on this thrilling journey. For in the world of day trading, anything is possible, and the rewards are beyond measure.

It's time to "Unleash the Hidden Trader Within" – You.

Congratulations on your decision to unleash the hidden trader within you!

By taking this step, you have already shown that you have the potential to become a successful trader and achieve financial freedom.

But let me tell you, this path is not for the faint-hearted. To succeed as a day trader, you need to put in the time and effort to learn the ropes before you can start earning.

Fortunately, Trading with Tarun is here to guide you every step of the way. With their expertly crafted, step-by-step guide, you will be able to fast-track your journey towards success.

By following the Day Trader Certification Steps and Strategies outlined in this guide, you will be able to transform your trading style and gain a competitive edge in the market.

So, let's begin this exciting journey by learning the basic rules for successful trading. Get ready to embark on a learning journey that will help you achieve your goals and unlock your full potential as a day trader.

CHAPTER 9
TRADING RULES FOR ALL BEGINNERS

Golden Rule No. 1 - Keeping a Trading Journal

In the world of trading, success often seems elusive. Despite our best efforts, we struggle to turn a consistent profit in the markets. We read books, attend courses, and follow the advice of experts, but still, we fall short.

But what if there was a tool that could help us unlock the secrets of successful trading? A tool that could help us analyze our performance, identify patterns in our behavior, and make the necessary changes to become profitable traders?

Enter the trading journal.

In my years of experience as a trader, I have found that keeping a trading journal is one of the most powerful tools in a trader's arsenal. By recording all of your trades, including the reasons for entering a trade, your emotions during the trade, and the outcome of the trade, you can gain valuable insights into your trading behavior.

At first, it might seem like just another task to add to your already lengthy to-do list. But the benefits of a trading journal are many. Not only can it help you analyze your past performance and identify areas for improvement, but it can also help you stay disciplined and focused on your goals.

By recording your reasons for entering a trade and your thought process during the trade, you can stay accountable to yourself and ensure that you're following your trading plan. And by looking back at your past trades, you can learn from your mistakes and successes, ultimately becoming a better and more confident trader.

So, if you're serious about becoming a successful trader, I urge you to start keeping a trading journal today. It could be the game-changing tool that helps you achieve your trading goals and become a profitable trader.

Golden Rule No. 2 - Follow the LETS approach.

1. L – Logic in the trade

In the world of trading, markets can be volatile, unpredictable, and unforgiving. But there's one trait that separates successful traders from the rest: logic.

Logic is the foundation of successful trading. It's the ability to use reason, analysis, and critical thinking to make informed trading decisions based on available data and market conditions. Without logic, traders may make impulsive and emotionally-driven trades, leading to losses and missed opportunities.

If you're serious about becoming a successful trader, I urge you to develop your logic and critical thinking skills. It could be the game-changing trait that helps you achieve your trading goals and become a profitable trader.

You have taken the trade because your friend got a tip from a third person. This should not be the basis of your trade as it is not logical, but rather gambling. Always remember, 'Tips are for waiters in restaurants, not for traders in the stock market.'

2. E – Entry

In the world of trading, timing is everything, and nowhere is this more apparent than in the importance of the right entry. The entry point is the moment when a trader buys or sells an asset, and getting it right can be the difference between a profitable trade and a loss.

By mastering the art of timing, you can increase your profit potential, minimize your risk exposure, and become a more confident and disciplined trader.

Always remember, and do not run behind the trade. Let the market come to your entry level always. If you have analyzed and identified one entry level, make sure you follow that. If the buying levels are gone, then leave the trade and grab the opportunity in some other trade rather than taking the wrong or late entry.

3. T – Target

The world of trading is full of excitement and adventure, but it can also be unforgiving for those who enter it without a clear plan. One of the most crucial aspects of a successful trading plan is setting clear targets. Targets help traders stay focused on their goals, and they play a significant role in determining the ultimate success of a trade.

Imagine you're a trader who's been studying the markets for months, analyzing charts, and studying technical indicators. You've identified a potential trade that meets your criteria, but before you enter it, you need to know where you plan to exit and take your profits. Without a target, you'd be trading blindly, hoping for the best, which is never a good strategy.

Setting a target provides a clear objective for your trade. It allows you to calculate your risk-reward ratio, which is a fundamental aspect of trading. Your risk-reward ratio is the amount of money you're willing to risk for each dollar you plan to make. By setting a target, you're essentially defining your risk and reward, which helps you make informed decisions.

Another reason why setting a target is important is that it helps you manage your emotions. Trading can be an emotional roller coaster, and without a target, you may find yourself making impulsive decisions based on fear or greed. Setting a target provides a rational basis for your decision-making and helps you avoid emotional trading.

4. S- Stop loss

Trading is like walking a tightrope – one wrong move can lead to a fall. The key to succeeding in this high-stakes game is to have a safety net in place, and that safety net is the stop loss.

Picture this: You've spent weeks analyzing the market, studying charts, and reading the news. You've finally found the perfect trade - the one that's going to make you a fortune. You enter the trade with high hopes, but then the unexpected happens. The market turns against you, and your profits turn into losses. You panic, hesitate, and before you know it, you've lost more than you can afford.

This scenario is all too common among traders, but it can be avoided with the help of a stop loss. A stop loss is a predetermined exit point that you set before entering a trade. It's your safety net, your insurance policy against unexpected market movements.

Setting a stop loss is not only essential for limiting your losses but also for managing your emotions. Emotions can be a trader's worst enemy, leading to irrational decisions and impulsive trades. When you set a stop loss, you're taking the emotion out of the equation and sticking to your plan.

But setting a stop loss is not enough – you need to set it at the right level. Too close, and you risk getting stopped out prematurely. Too far, and you risk losing more than you can afford. The key is to find the sweet spot – the level that allows for some market volatility but also limits your potential losses.

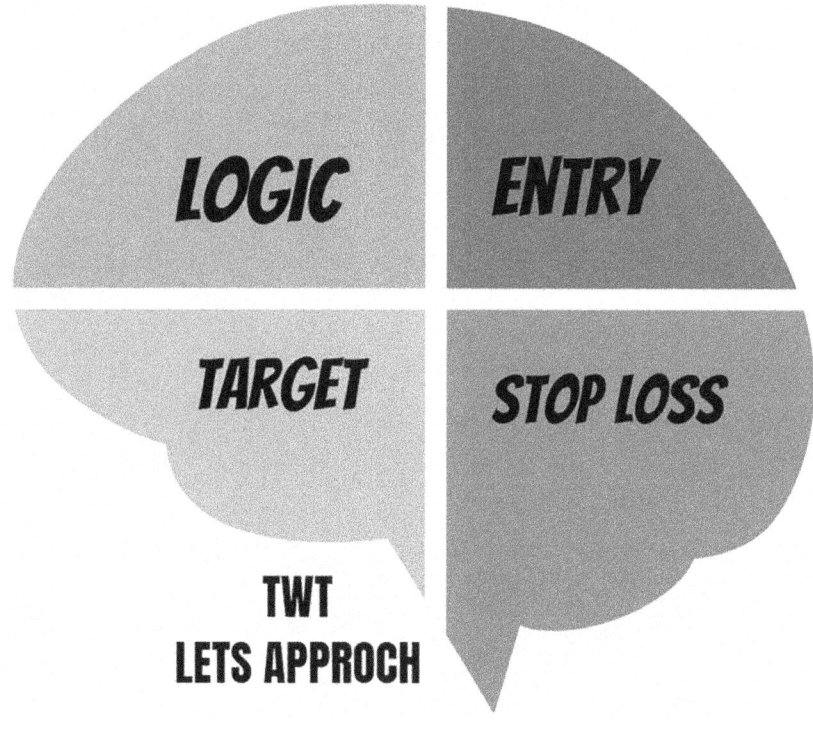

CHAPTER

10 DIFFERENT STAGES FOR TRADERS

Are you a beginner trader looking to make a fortune in the stock market? Or maybe you've been trading for a while and are struggling to turn a profit. Regardless of where you are in your trading journey, understanding the different stages that traders go through can help you become a better trader and avoid common pitfalls.

So, what are these stages? Let's take a closer look.

Stage 1: Lucky Trader

The first stage of trading is the Lucky Trader stage, where beginners try their hand at trading for various reasons. Maybe they saw their friends making money, or perhaps they got inspired by social media influencers. Whatever the reason, new traders are often in for a pleasant surprise when they make their first few trades. They may not have a solid trading strategy, but they still manage to make some money, thanks to what's commonly known as "beginner's luck."

But here's the catch: when you're new to trading, it's easy to get carried away by the excitement and start dreaming of making a fortune overnight. You may even start to believe that you're some sort of trading prodigy who doesn't need to follow any rules or have a solid trading plan. Unfortunately, this is where most traders go wrong. Once the excitement dies down, they realize that they've lost a considerable amount of money.

Stage 2: Curious Soul

The second stage of trading is the Curious Soul stage. This is where traders start to wonder how other people are making money in the market and start to look for tips and calls. Unfortunately, this is a dangerous path to take. As the saying goes, "tips belong to waiters in restaurants, not for traders in the stock market." Most traders who fall into this trap end up losing even more money and start to hate the stock market and other traders. At this point, they may decide that trading is not for them and quit.

Stage 3: Learning is Earning.

The third stage of trading is the Learning is Earning stage. This is where traders realize that there is no earning without learning. They understand that they need to learn the art of trading before they can make consistent profits. They start to learn by joining trading workshops, watching YouTube videos, reading books, and so on. They also start to recover their lost money slowly by following proper risk and money management. This is a crucial stage for any trader who wants to make a living from trading.

Stage 4: Self-Proclaimed Master

The fourth and final stage of trading is the Self-Proclaimed Master stage. This is where traders think they've got it all figured out and start to experiment with new trading strategies. They may even start to give tips and calls to their friends and family, but to their surprise, they start to make losses when they trade on their own. This is a tough stage to get out of, and most traders are trapped in it forever. The only way to get out of this stage is to find a true mentor or coach who can guide you and help you stay focused on your trading goals.

Stage 5: The Independent Trader

The ultimate destination for every aspiring trader is the coveted Independent Trader stage. Having weathered the ups and downs of the market, these individuals have honed their skills, developed a robust trading plan, and acquired the necessary knowledge to navigate the intricate web of stocks. They possess the self-assurance and expertise to trade autonomously, making informed decisions and seizing opportunities with precision.

So, there you have it - the different stages of trading. Remember, every stage is unique and can teach you something new about trading. By understanding these stages, you can avoid common mistakes and become a better trader. Good luck on your trading journey!

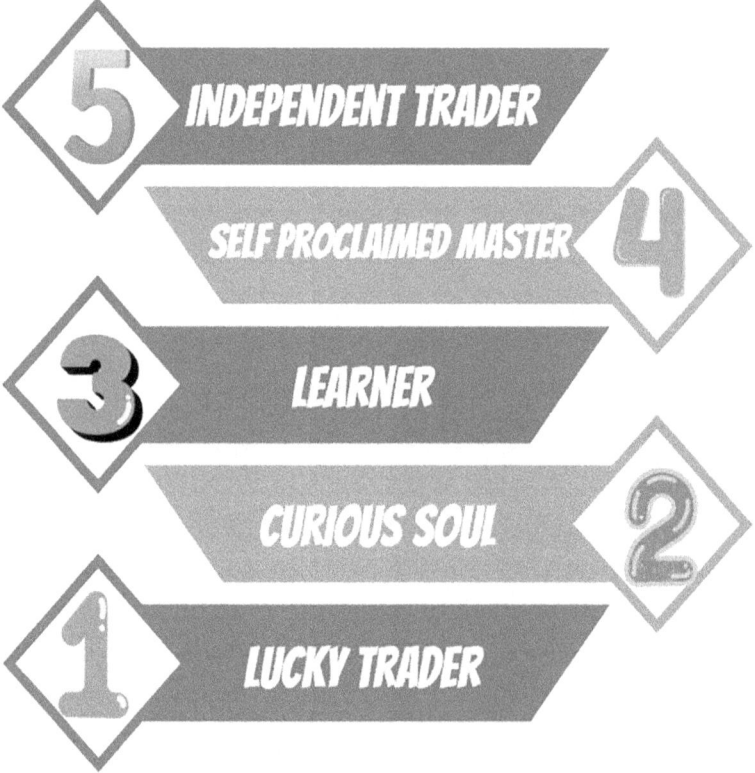

By taking the decision to read this book and learn, you have already upgraded your level and TWT promises you that learning before earning is the only way to make long-term wealth. So let's start the journey with the basics of trading, which every profitable and independent trader must know.

CHAPTER 11

DECODING PRICE ACTION: THE HIDDEN LANGUAGE OF THE MARKETS

Welcome to the thrilling world of price action, where charts come alive and tell tales of triumph and intrigue. In this book, we'll embark on an exhilarating journey, peeling back the layers to uncover the secrets of the markets and empower you to make smarter trading decisions.

Imagine this: You're sitting in front of your trading screen, watching the price bars paint a vivid picture of market movements. The way these bars form, the patterns they create, and the way they interact with support and resistance levels—it's like a language waiting to be understood. And that's exactly what price action trading is all about.

Price action strips away the complexity of countless indicators and focuses on what truly matters—the price itself. It's like learning a new language, where each candlestick and each swing on the chart tells a story. By mastering this language, you'll gain a deeper understanding of market dynamics and gain a significant edge in your trading journey.

But let's not forget the human element. Price action is not just about numbers on a screen; it's about the emotions and actions of traders. Behind every price movement lies greed, fear, hope, and uncertainty. Price action traders become like detectives, deciphering these emotions to anticipate potential market turns and trends.

What makes price action truly captivating is its versatility. Whether you're a short-term trader looking for quick gains or a long-term investor seeking value, price action adapts to your trading style. It is like a universal tool that helps you navigate the markets with confidence and precision.

However, do not be fooled by its apparent simplicity. Mastering price action requires dedication and practice. It is a skill that develops over time as you immerse yourself in the charts, study historical patterns, and learn from experience. It is a journey that tests your patience, resilience, and ability to keep emotions in check.

But fear not, dear reader, for the rewards are well worth the effort. By delving into the art of price action, you unlock a new level of understanding and gain the power to interpret the market's secret language. You become an architect of your own trading destiny, making informed decisions based on what the charts are telling you.

In this book, I invite you to join me in unraveling the mysteries of price action—the key to unlocking the secrets of the markets. Get ready for a thrilling adventure as we navigate the ups and downs, decode the hidden messages, and unleash the power of price action. Brace yourself for a transformative journey that will forever change the way you approach trading.

LANGUAGE OF CHARTS: CANDLESTICK PATTERNS

When it comes to reading a chart in the trading world, there are numerous methods available to you. You can use techniques such as Japanese Candlestick Patterns, Renko, Bar, Line, Heikin Ashi, Point & Figure, and many others. The question on your mind may be, which one should you choose?

In my experience, the most popular and effective approach is Candlestick Patterns. The reason is simple: it's easy to learn, and it works. That's why I have crafted this comprehensive guide to teach you everything you need to know about Candlestick Patterns, including how to trade like a pro.

In this guide, you will learn:

- What is a candlestick pattern and how do you read it correctly?
- Bullish reversal candlestick patterns and how to find high probability setups
- Bearish reversal candlestick patterns and how to find high probability setups.
- Indecision candlestick patterns.
- Trend continuation candlestick patterns and how to find high probability setups
- How to understand any candlestick pattern using a cheat sheet.

This is an extensive guide on candlestick patterns, so take your time to digest the material and return to it whenever you need a refresher. With this knowledge, you'll be equipped to read charts using candlestick patterns with ease and confidence. Let's begin this journey together!

WHAT IS A CANDLESTICK PATTERN?

The world of trading and investing can be a daunting place. With so many different strategies and techniques to choose from, it can be difficult to know where to start. However, one technique that has stood the test of time is Japanese candlestick charting.

It all began in the 1700s with a Japanese rice trader named Munehisa Homma. Homma used candlestick charts to track the price movements of rice, a technique that allowed him to visualize the market like never before. By identifying patterns in the price movements, Homma was able to make predictions about future price changes, giving him a significant advantage over other traders.

Flash forward 300 years and the art of Japanese candlestick charting has become a staple in the world of trading and investing. Steve Nison, the author of Japanese Candlestick Charting Techniques, introduced the technique to the Western world. This proved to be a turning point, as traders and investors were able to gain insight into market movements in a way they had never experienced before.

So, what exactly is a candlestick chart? Imagine a graph where each candlestick represents a specific time period, such as a day or an hour. The body of the candlestick shows the opening and closing prices for that time period, while the wicks or shadows represent the highest and lowest prices. By studying these patterns, traders and investors can gain insights into the price movements of a particular asset and make more informed trading decisions.

In other words, candlestick charting is more than just a chart - it's a window into the market's behavior. By learning how to read and interpret candlestick charts, traders and investors can gain a deeper understanding of market trends and use this knowledge to their advantage.

SO, HOW DO YOU READ A JAPANESE CANDLESTICK CHART?

Now, every candlestick pattern has four data points: O.H.L.C.

- Open – The opening price
- High – The highest price during a fixed time period.
- Low – The lowest price over a fixed time period
- Close – The closing price

Here's what I mean:

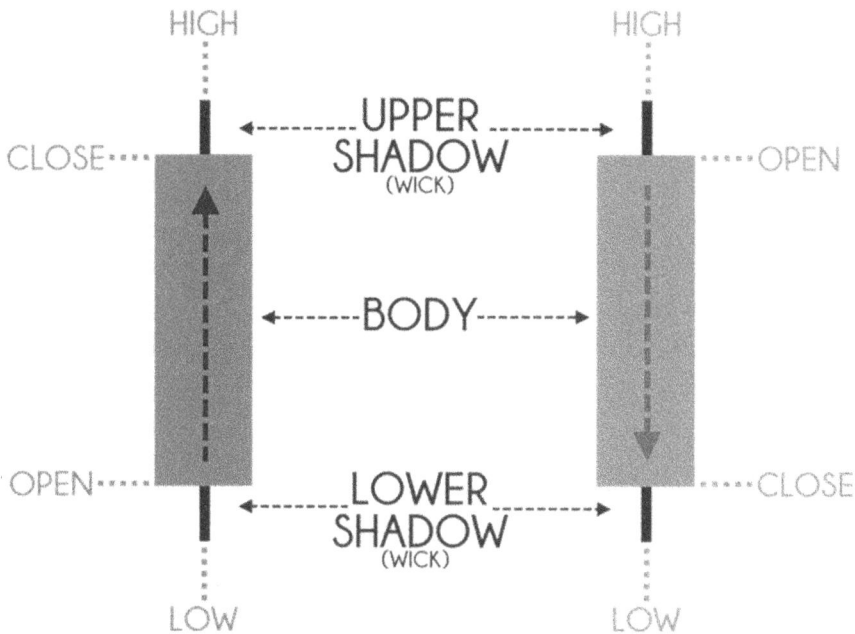

Remember...

For a Bullish candle, the open is always BELOW the close. For a Bearish candle, the open is always ABOVE the close.

BULLISH REVERSAL CANDLESTICK PATTERNS

If you are new to trading and trying to figure out how to read candlestick charts, you might have heard of bullish reversal candlestick patterns. But what do they really mean, and how can you use them to your advantage?

First things first, a bullish reversal candlestick pattern signals a temporary shift in the market's momentum. This means that buyers are momentarily in control, but it doesn't necessarily mean that the trend will continue. So, before you go long, it's important to combine candlestick patterns with other tools to find a high probability trading setup.

Now, let's talk about five bullish reversal candlestick patterns that you should know:

- Hammer
- Bullish Engulfing Pattern
- Piercing Pattern
- Tweezer Bottom
- Morning Star

Let me explain…

HAMMER

This pattern appears at the end of a downtrend and signals a potential reversal. It has a small real body at the top and a long lower wick, indicating that buyers have stepped in to push the price back up.

Here's how to recognize it:

- There is little to no upper shadow.
- The price closes at the top 1/4 of the range.

The lower shadow is about two or three times the length of the body.

And this is what a hammer means…

- When the market opened, the sellers took control and pushed the price lower.
- At the selling climax, huge buying pressure stepped in and pushed the price higher.

- The buying pressure is so strong that it closed above the opening price.

In short, a hammer is a bullish reversal candlestick pattern that shows rejection of lower prices.

If you spot a Hammer pattern, it is not a guarantee that the trend will reverse right away. To increase your chances of a successful trade, you need additional confirmation. Don't worry, I'll show you how to do this in detail later on. So, keep reading to learn more about the tools you can use to find high probability trading setups.

BULLISH ENGULFING PATTERN

The Bullish Engulfing Pattern is a popular bullish reversal pattern that traders use to identify potential buying opportunities. Here's how to spot it:

Look for a two-candle pattern.

- The first candle should be a bearish candlestick.
- The second candle should be a larger bullish candlestick that completely engulfs the previous bearish candle.
- The second candle should close near the high of the range.

This pattern is significant because it shows that buyers have overwhelmed sellers, pushing the price up and potentially signaling a shift in the trend. However, it is important to remember that this pattern alone is not enough to make a trading decision. It should be used in combination with other analyses and indicators to confirm a potential trade setup.

PIERCING PATTERN

The Piercing Pattern is another popular bullish reversal pattern that traders use to identify potential buying opportunities. Here's how to spot it:

Look for a two-candle pattern.

- The first candle should be a bearish candlestick.
- The second candle should be a larger bullish candlestick that opens below the low of the previous bearish candle.
- The second candle should close above the midpoint of the previous bearish candle.

This pattern is significant because it shows that buyers have stepped in after a bearish period and pushed the price up.

TWEEZER BOTTOM

The Tweezer Bottom is a bullish reversal pattern that traders use to identify potential buying opportunities. Here's how to spot it:

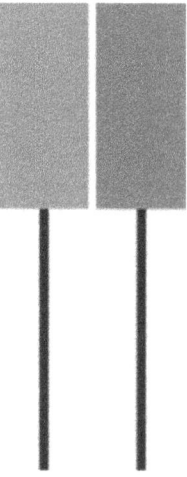

Look for two candlesticks with the same low price.

- The first candlestick should be a bearish candlestick.
- The second candlestick should be a bullish candlestick with a long lower shadow, indicating that buyers have pushed the price up.

This pattern is significant because it shows that the bears were unable to push the price down any further, and buyers have stepped in to push the price up.

MORNING STAR

The Morning Star is a bullish reversal pattern that traders use to identify potential buying opportunities. Here's how to spot it:

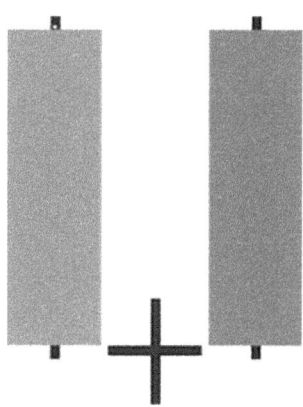

Look for a three-candle pattern.

The first candle should be a bearish candlestick.

The second candle should be a small-bodied candlestick that gaps down from the first candle.

The third candle should be a bullish candlestick that closes above the midpoint of the first candle.

This pattern is significant because it shows that the bears were in control, but the bulls have taken over and pushed the price up.

In short, a Morning Star indicates that the sellers are exhausted and the buyers are momentarily in control.

HOW TO FIND HIGH PROBABILITY BULLISH REVERSAL SETUPS

Congratulations! You are now familiar with the different bullish reversal candlestick patterns. But how can you use them to identify high probability trading setups?

Remember: Trading candlestick patterns in isolation will not give you an edge in the markets. To increase your chances of success, you need to combine them with other tools and techniques.

Here is a simple three-step process to follow:

Look for a trend in the market. If the trend is up, you want to be a buyer.

Wait for a pullback towards a level of support. This is where buyers are likely to step in and push the price higher.

Once the price reaches support, look for a bullish reversal candlestick pattern to confirm the trend reversal. But don't stop there! Make sure the size of the candlestick pattern is larger than previous candles, indicating a strong rejection of lower prices.

Here are a few cherry-picked examples:

MORNING STAR:

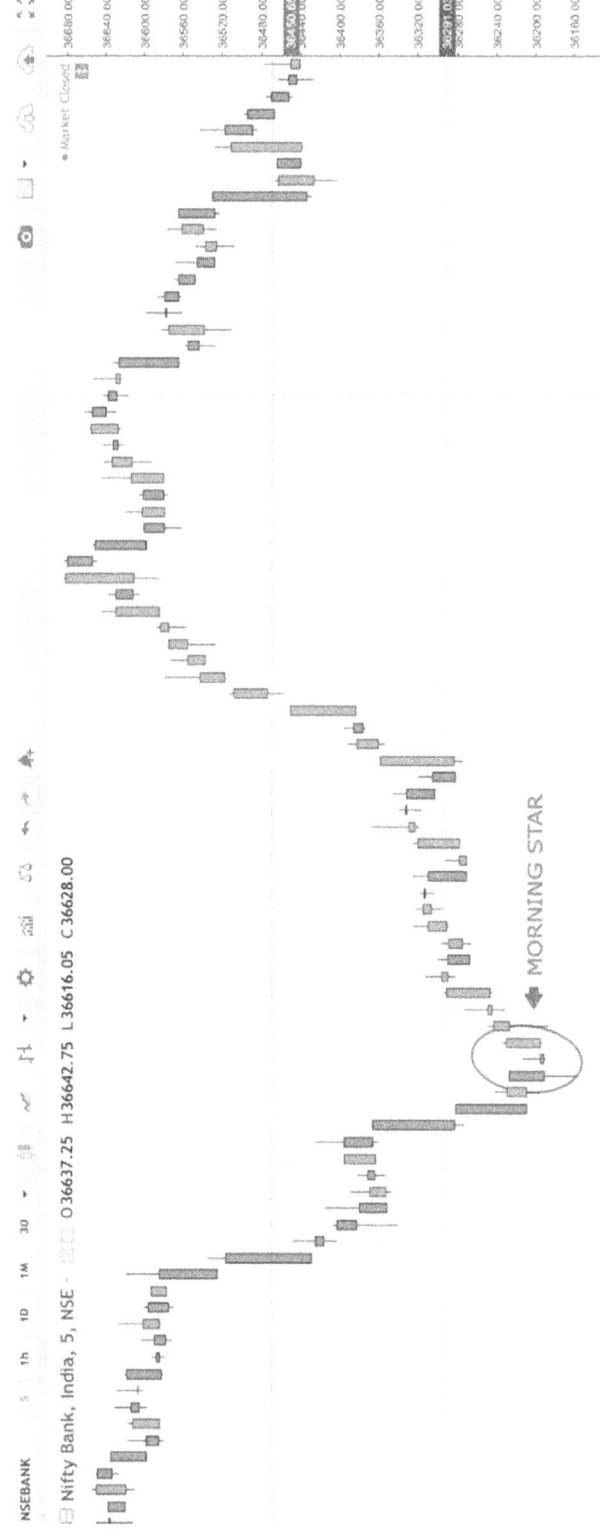

BULLISH ENGULFING PATTERN

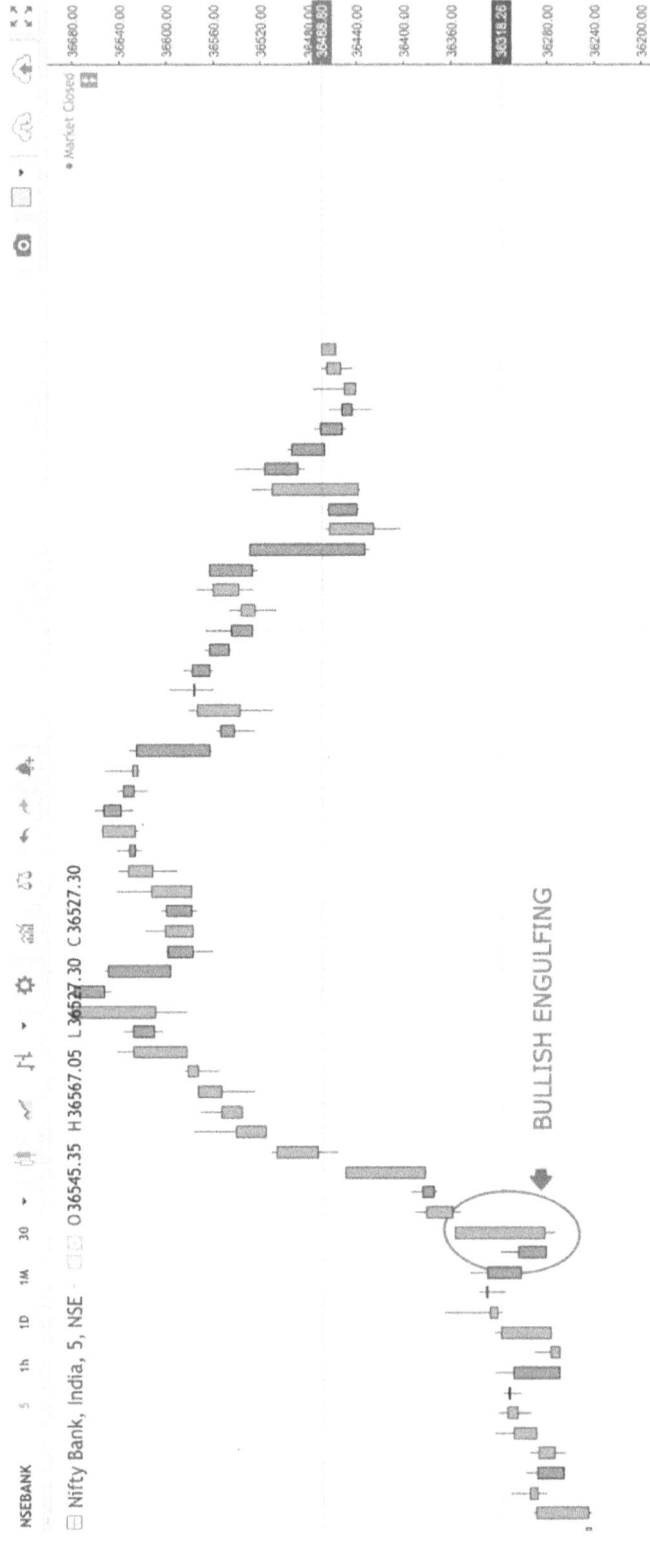

BULLISH ENGULFING PATTERN

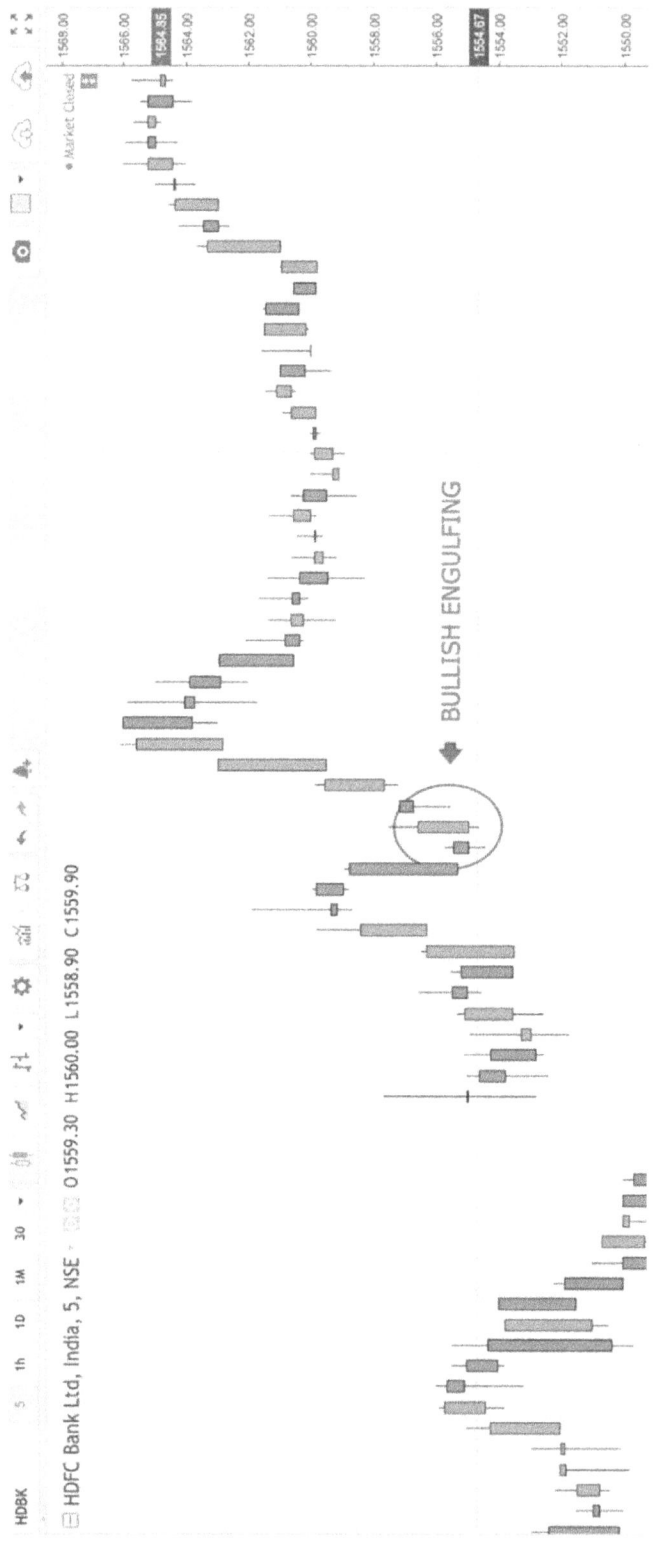

Note: There will be losing trades as well, and this is not the "holy grail".

By following these steps, you'll have a higher probability of catching a trend reversal and making a profitable trade. But as always, be sure to conduct further analysis and use risk management techniques to protect your capital.

BEARISH REVERSAL CANDLESTICK PATTERNS

After bullish reversal patterns, let me welcome you to the world of bearish reversal candlestick patterns! These patterns indicate that the sellers are taking charge of the market momentarily. But before you start shorting, let me tell you that spotting a bearish reversal pattern alone doesn't guarantee profitable trades. You need to combine it with other tools to find a high probability trading setup.

To get you started, here are five bearish reversal candlestick patterns that you should be aware of:

1. Shooting Star
2. Bearish Engulfing Pattern
3. Dark Cloud Cover
4. Tweezer Top
5. Evening Star

These patterns are not standalone signals for you to initiate a trade. You need to identify a few other factors before you take a position. Let me explain the process step-by-step.

SHOOTING STAR

The Shooting Star is a bearish reversal candlestick pattern that indicates the price may be about to reverse to the downside. Here's how to recognize it:

- The candlestick has a small real body, and a long upper shadow that is at least twice the length of the body.

- There is little to no lower shadow.
- The candlestick opens higher than the previous candle and closes near its low, indicating that the sellers have taken control.

In short, the Shooting Star shows that the buyers attempted to push the price higher, but the sellers stepped in and pushed it back down, resulting in a bearish sentiment.

BEARISH ENGULFING PATTERN

A bearish engulfing pattern is a two-candlestick pattern that indicates a possible trend reversal. It occurs when a small bullish candle is followed by a larger bearish candle that "engulfs" or completely covers the previous candle's body.

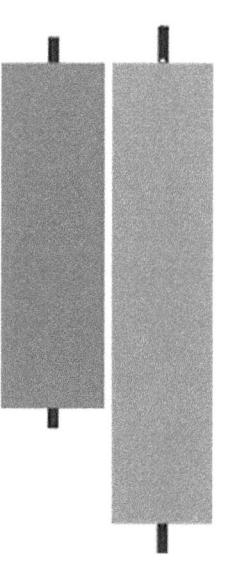

To locate a bearish engulfing pattern, look for the following characteristics on a candlestick chart:

- The first candle is a bullish candle, which means it opens at a lower price and closes at a higher price.
- The second candle is a bearish candle that opens higher than the previous candle's close and then closes lower than the previous candle's open.
- The second candle fully engulfs the first candle, meaning its body completely covers the body of the first candle.
- The larger the second candle is compared to the first candle, the more significant the pattern becomes.
- It's essential t

In essence, a Bearish Engulfing Pattern tells you the sellers have overwhelmed the buyers and are now in control.

DARK CLOUD COVER

Dark Cloud Cover is a bearish reversal candlestick pattern that consists of two candles. The first candle is bullish and the second candle is bearish. The bearish candle opens above the previous day's high but then closes below the midpoint of the previous day's bullish candle. This pattern indicates a potential reversal of the bullish trend and suggests that the bears are taking control.

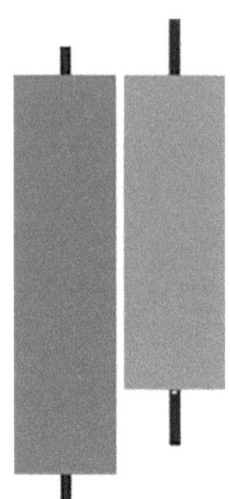

Here's how you can locate it:

- Look for an uptrend in the price chart.
- Wait for a bullish candlestick to form, signaling the continuation of the uptrend.
- Then, look for a bearish candlestick to form the next day, opening above the previous day's high and closing below the previous day's midpoint.
- This bearish candlestick is the Dark Cloud Cover pattern, indicating a potential reversal of the previous uptrend.

TWEEZER TOP

The Tweezer Top is a bearish reversal candlestick pattern that consists of two candlesticks with almost the same high price. It suggests that the market has reached a potential top and the bullish trend may be losing momentum. The pattern is formed by:

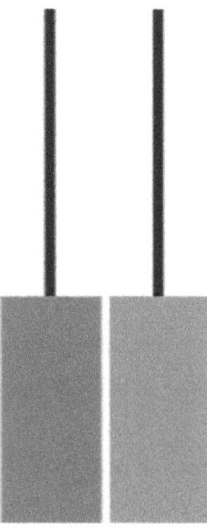

The first candlestick is a bullish candlestick, which means that the price opened lower than the previous day's close but closed higher than the open.

The second candlestick is a bearish candlestick, which means that the price opened higher than the previous day's close but closed lower than the open.

Both candlesticks have almost the same high price, forming a horizontal line that represents resistance.

To locate the Tweezer Top pattern, you need to look for two candlesticks with almost the same high price. This means that the wicks of the two candlesticks should be at the same level or very close to each other. The candlesticks can have different lengths, but the important thing is that they have almost the same high price. When you spot this pattern, it could be a sign that the bullish trend is losing momentum and the bears may take over.

EVENING STAR

"The Evening Star" is a bearish reversal candlestick pattern that consists of three candles:

1. The first candle is a bullish candlestick, indicating that buyers are in control of the market.
2. The second candle is a small-bodied candlestick, indicating indecision in the market.
3. The third candle is a bearish candlestick, indicating that sellers have taken control of the market.

To identify the Evening Star pattern:

- Look for a bullish candlestick.

Followed by a small-bodied candlestick that gaps up.

- Followed by a bearish candlestick that gaps down and closes below the midpoint of the first candle's body.

The Evening Star pattern is a strong indication of a trend reversal, suggesting that the uptrend is losing momentum and the bears are taking control.

HOW TO FIND HIGH PROBABILITY BEARISH REVERSAL SETUPS

Congratulations on learning the different bearish reversal candlestick patterns! But now it's time to take it to the next level and learn how to identify high probability trading opportunities using these patterns.

Here's a step-by-step guide:

- If the market is trending downwards, wait for a pullback towards resistance.
- Once the price has pulled back to resistance, keep an eye out for a bearish reversal candlestick pattern.
- If you spot a bearish reversal candlestick pattern, make sure it is larger than the previous candles to signal strong rejection.
- If the candlestick pattern shows strong rejection, go short on the next candle's open.
- For long setups, simply follow the same steps but in reverse.
- By combining these candlestick patterns with other tools, you can increase your chances of finding profitable trades.

Here are a few cherry-picked examples:

BEARISH ENGULFING PATTERN

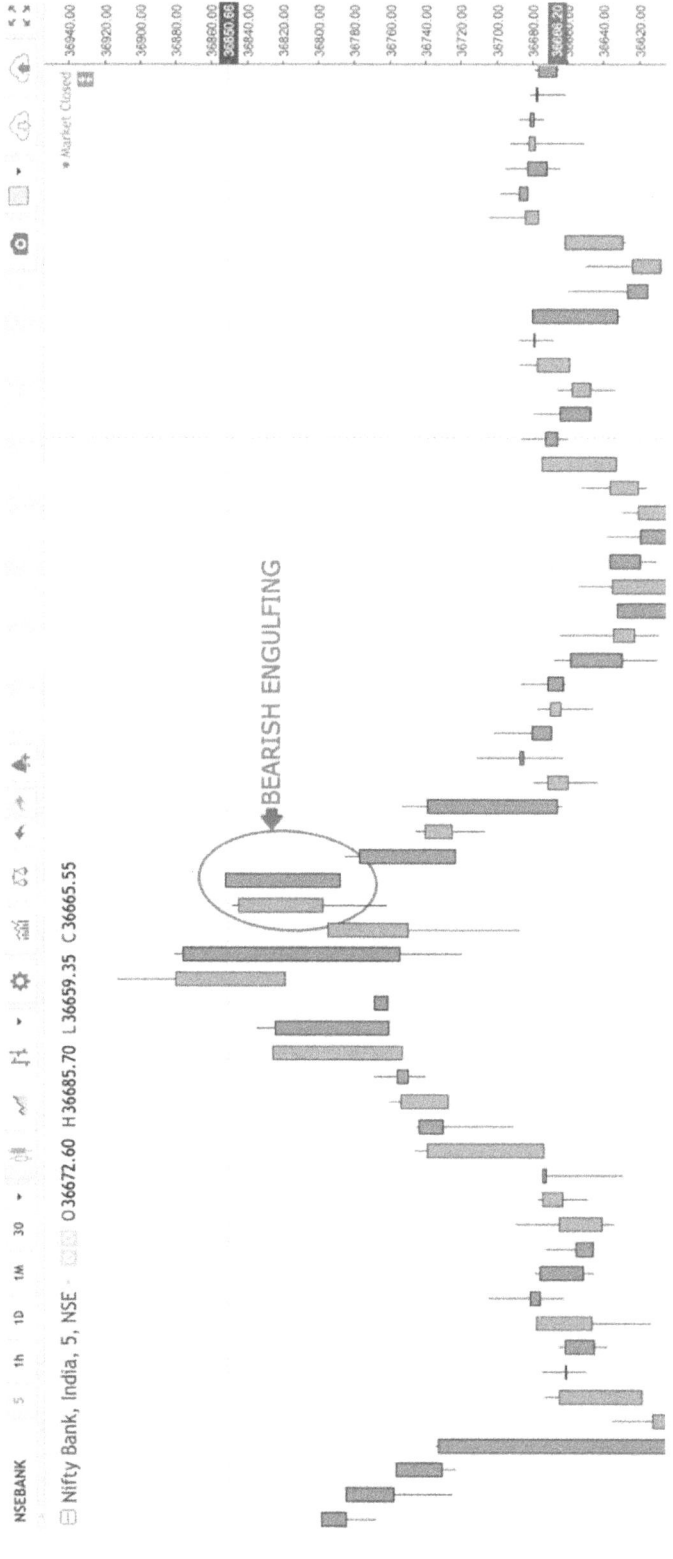

SHOOTING STAR

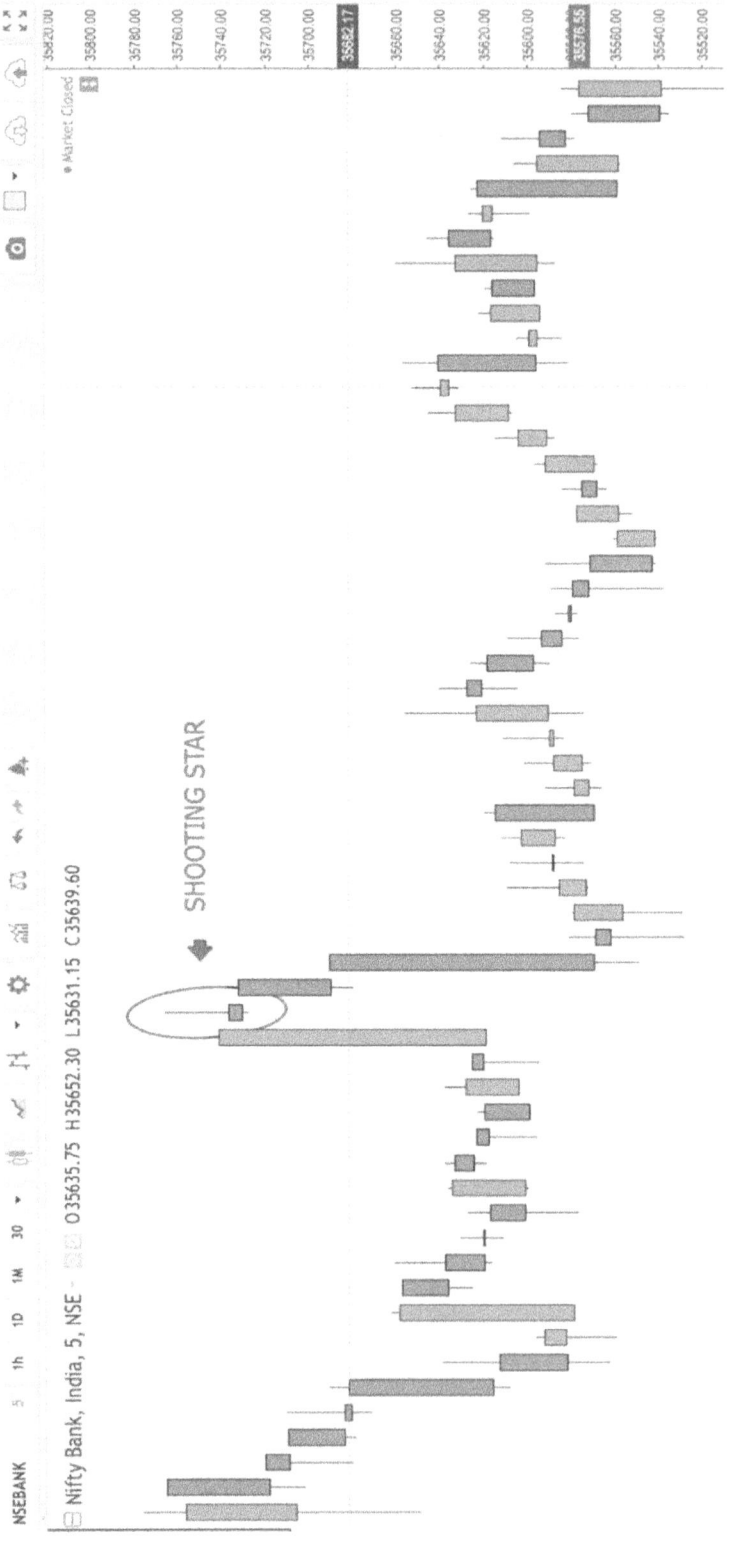

Note: There will be losing trades as well, and this is not the "holy grail".

INDECISION CANDLESTICK PATTERNS

Have you ever looked at a candlestick chart and felt unsure about what the market is trying to tell you? That's where indecision candlestick patterns come in. These patterns indicate that the market is undecided and could go either way. The patterns are: -

- Doji and
- Spinning Top,

But don't let that uncertainty discourage you from trading. In fact, indecision candlestick patterns can be a powerful tool when used in combination with other technical analysis tools. For example, if you see a Doji after a strong uptrend, it could signal a potential reversal. Or, if you see a series of Spinning Tops, it could indicate a possible consolidation period before the market makes its next move.

Let me explain in detail...

SPINNING TOP

The Spinning Top pattern is an indecision candlestick pattern that indicates a tug-of-war between buyers and sellers. This pattern suggests that neither buyers nor sellers are in control of the market, and that a potential trend reversal or continuation is possible.

How to locate a Spinning Top.

- Look for a candlestick with a small real body.

The upper and lower shadows should be roughly equal in length and twice the size of the real body.

- The color of the real body is not important, it can be bullish or bearish
- The spinning top pattern indicates indecision in the market and suggests that neither buyers nor sellers are in control

- It is best to wait for confirmation from subsequent price action before making a trading decision.

DOJI

A Doji is a single candlestick pattern that signifies indecision in the market. It occurs when the opening and closing prices are the same or very close, resulting in a small body and long shadows. The pattern looks like a cross or a plus sign.

There are several ways to locate a Doji candlestick pattern:

- Look for a candlestick with a small body, where the opening and closing prices are almost equal.
- The wicks or shadows of the candlestick can be short or long.
- The Doji can appear in both bullish and bearish markets, indicating indecision in the market.
- Dojis can occur on any time frame, so check different time frames to identify them.
- It's important to consider the context in which the Doji occurs, such as the trend and previous price action, to determine its significance.

Although Doji is an indecisive candlestick pattern, there are variations with different significances.

They are:
- Dragonfly Doji
- Gravestone Doji

1. Dragonfly Doji

A Dragonfly Doji is a candlestick pattern that forms when the opening and closing prices of an asset are almost identical and occur at the high of the trading range. The pattern resembles a "T" shape and signifies indecision in the market. Here's how to locate a Dragonfly Doji pattern:

Look for a candlestick with a long lower shadow and little to no upper shadow.

- The opening and closing prices should be close to the high of the trading range.
- The color of the candlestick doesn't matter, as long as it meets the above criteria.

If you spot a Dragonfly Doji pattern, it could indicate that the market is undecided and a potential reversal could occur.

2. Gravestone Doji

A Gravestone Doji pattern is a candlestick pattern that indicates indecision in the market and can potentially signal a bearish reversal. It is characterized by a long upper shadow, little or no lower shadow, and a small real body near the bottom of the price range. Here's how to locate it:

- Look for a doji candlestick pattern with a long upper shadow and little or no lower shadow.
- The opening and closing of the candlestick should be near the bottom of the price range, indicating that sellers are in control.

The candlestick should appear after an uptrend, potentially signaling a bearish reversal.

CONTINUATION CANDLESTICK PATTERNS

If you are a trader who loves to trade trends and wants to learn about candlestick patterns that can help you take advantage of the market's momentum, you're in luck because we're about to cover some of the most reliable continuation patterns out there.

As the name suggests, continuation patterns indicate that the market is likely to keep moving in the same direction, making them particularly useful for trend traders. So, without further ado, here are the four continuation patterns you should know:

- Rising Three Method
- Falling Three Method
- Bullish Harami
- Bearish Harami

Let's dive in and find out more about these powerful trading tools!

RISING THREE METHOD

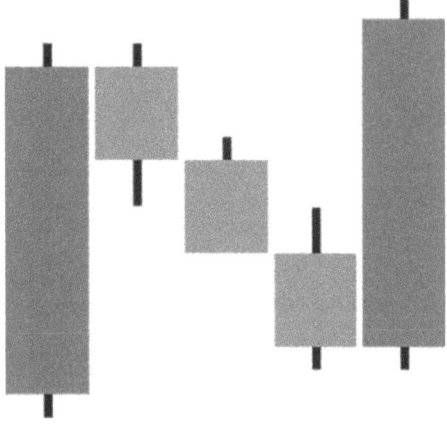

The Rising Three Method is a bullish continuation candlestick pattern that forms during an uptrend. This pattern indicates that despite some short-term selling pressure, buyers are still in control, and the uptrend is likely to continue. The three small bearish candlesticks represent a brief pause or consolidation in the market before the buyers step back in and push prices higher.

Steps to locate a Rising Three Method pattern:

- Look for an established uptrend in the market.
- The first candlestick in the pattern should be a long bullish candle.
- The next three candlesticks should be relatively small bearish candles that trade within the range of the first candlestick.

- The fifth candlestick should be another long bullish candle that closes above the high of the first candlestick, confirming the continuation of the uptrend.
- Keep an eye out for confirmation of the pattern by looking for high trading volumes during the fifth candlestick.

FALLING THREE METHOD

The Falling Three Method is a bearish continuation pattern that occurs in a downtrend.

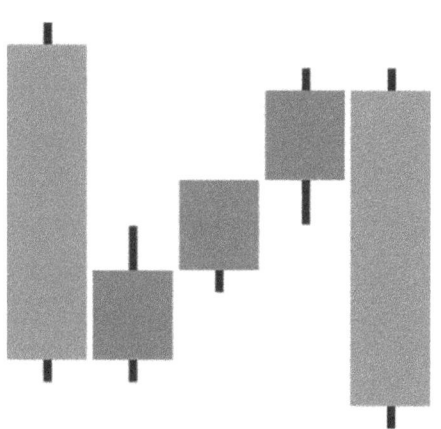

Here's how to identify it:

- The first candlestick in the pattern must be a long bearish candlestick.
- The next three candlesticks must be small bullish candlesticks, which are also called "rising windows."
- These three candlesticks must be contained within the high and low range of the first candlestick.
- The last candlestick in the pattern must be a long bearish candlestick, which closes below the low of the three small bullish candlesticks.

If these conditions are met, it suggests that the downtrend is likely to continue.

BULLISH HARAMI

The Bullish Harami pattern is a two-candlestick pattern that suggests a potential reversal of a downtrend.

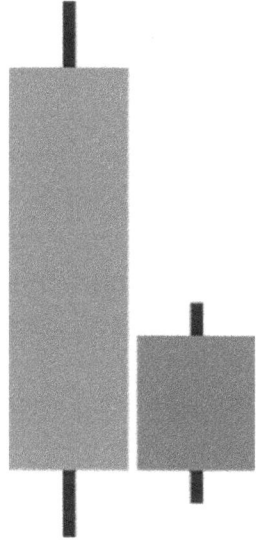

The first candlestick is a long bearish candle, followed by a smaller bullish candle that is completely within the range of the previous candle.

This pattern shows that the selling pressure is decreasing, and the bulls are starting to take control.

How to locate a bullish Harami pattern:

- Look for a downtrend in the market.
- Locate a long red (bearish) candlestick.
- The next day, look for a smaller green (bullish) candlestick that is completely within the range of the previous day's candlestick.
- The smaller green candlestick signals indecision in the market and a potential reversal of the downtrend.
- If the following day confirms the reversal with another green candlestick, it could be a good opportunity to go long.
- Note: You can treat the Harami as an inside bar. They mean the same thing and can be traded in a similar context.

BEARISH HARAMI

The bearish harami pattern is a two-candlestick pattern that signals a potential reversal of an uptrend. It is characterized by a small bullish candlestick, followed by a larger bearish candlestick that is completely engulfed by the previous candle's body. The bearish harami pattern suggests that buying pressure is waning and that the bears are gaining control.

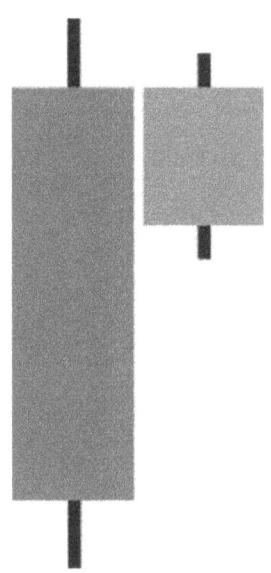

To locate a bearish harami pattern, follow these steps:

- Look for an uptrend in the market.

- Identify a long bullish candlestick.
- Look for a small bullish candlestick that appears next to the long bullish candlestick.
- Make sure that the small bullish candlestick is completely engulfed by the body of the next bearish candlestick.
- This bearish candlestick confirms the bearish harami pattern and signals a potential reversal of the uptrend.

HOW TO FIND HIGH PROBABILITY TREND CONTINUATION SETUPS

Congratulations on learning about continuation candlestick patterns! Now, let's take it up a notch and learn how to spot high probability trading opportunities with these patterns. Here's your step-by-step guide:

- Look for a market that is trading in a range and wait for it to break out of resistance.
- Once the market breaks out of resistance, keep a lookout for continuation candlestick patterns such as the Rising Three Method or Bullish Harami.
- If you spot a continuation candlestick pattern, make sure to go long on the break of the highs.
- And, of course, the opposite applies for short setups.

By following these steps, you'll be well on your way to spotting profitable trading opportunities with continuation candlestick patterns. Happy trading!

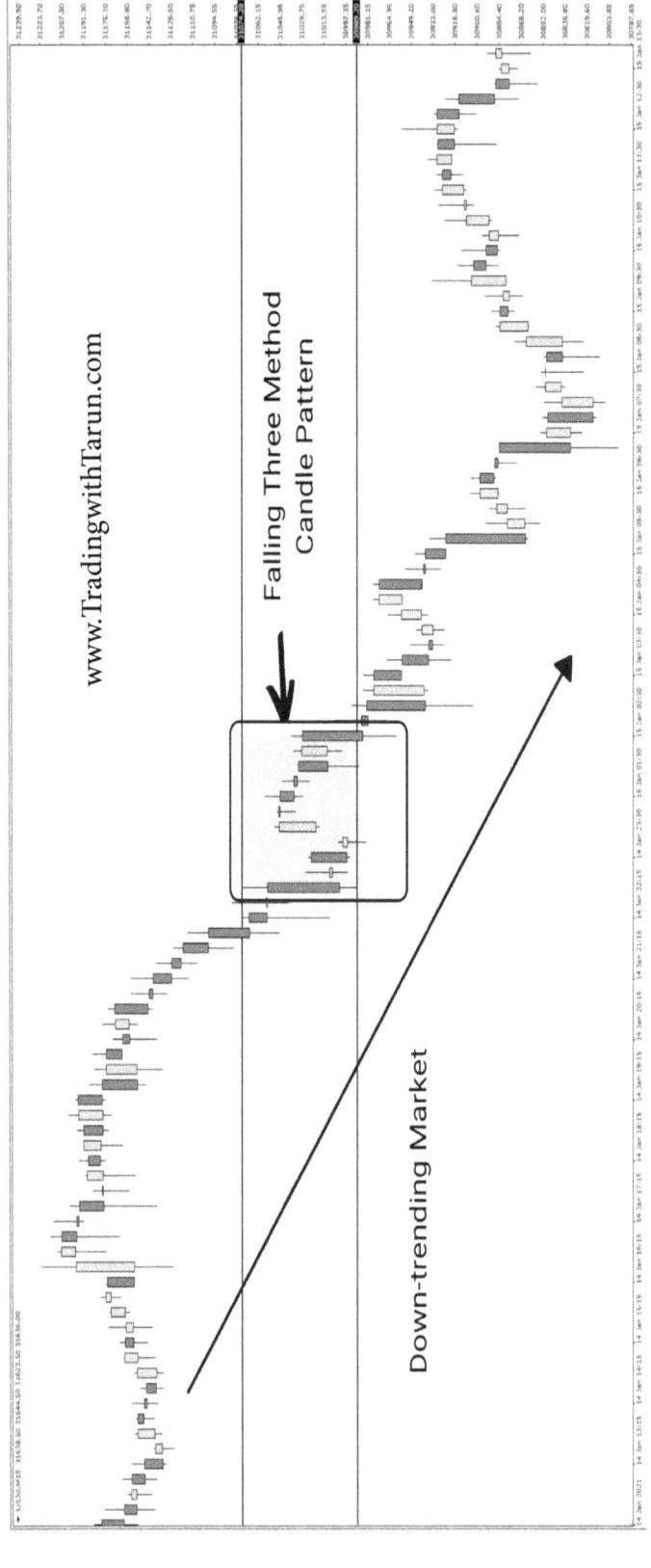

RISING THREE METHOD AND BULLISH HARAMI ON BANK NIFTY

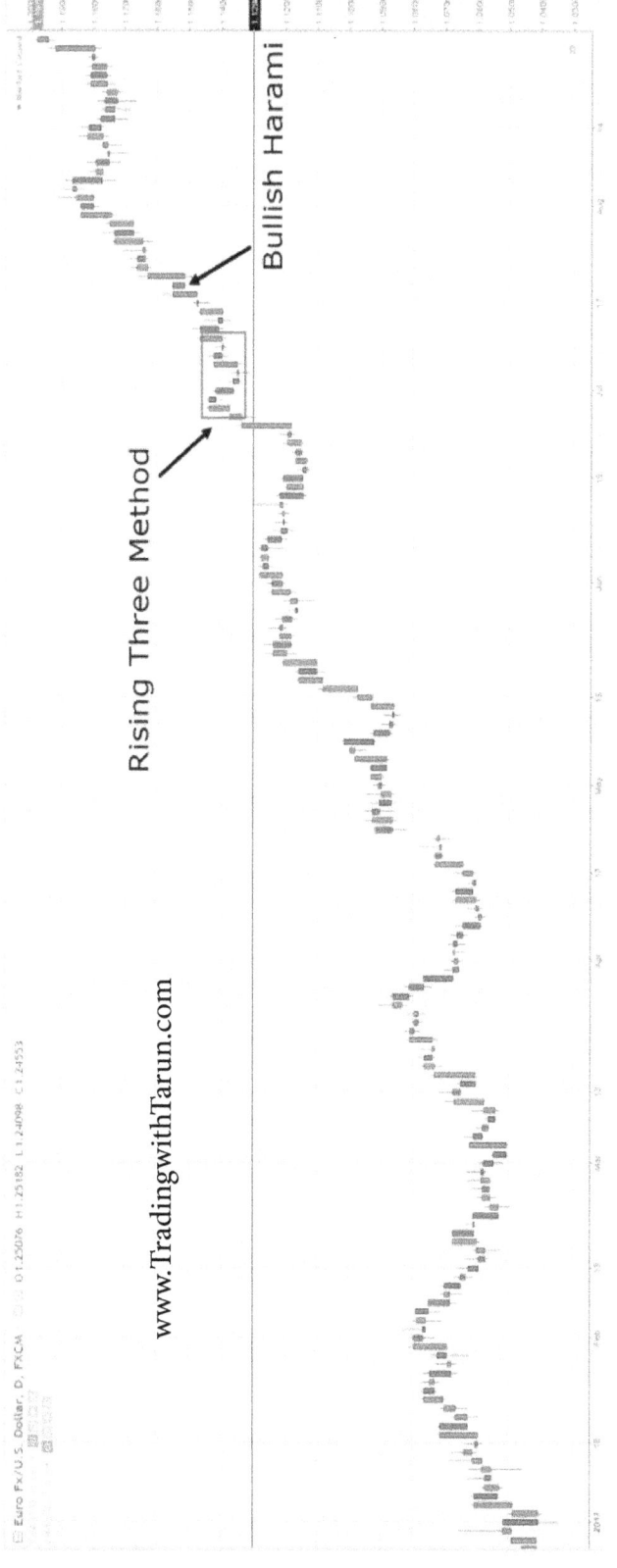

RISING THREE METHOD AND BULLISH HARAMI ON BANK NIFTY

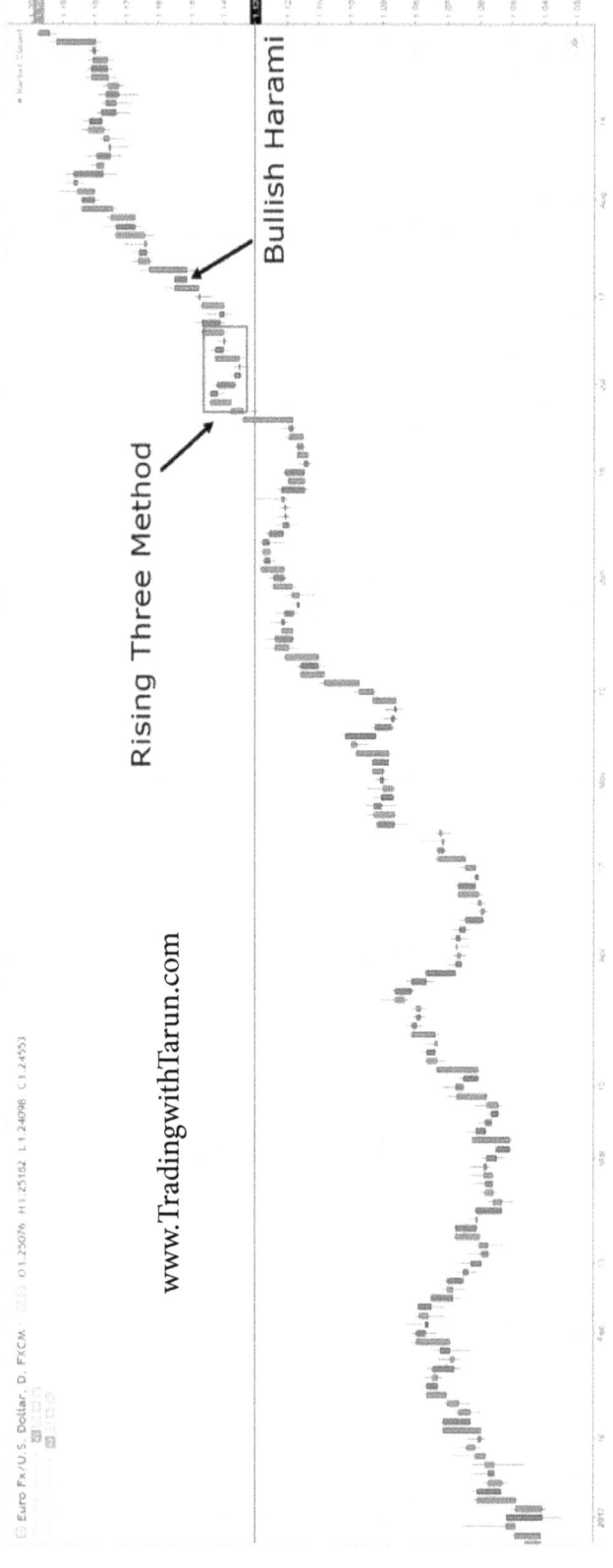

This is powerful stuff, right? Great!

Let's move on…

CANDLESTICK PATTERNS CHEAT SHEET: HOW TO UNDERSTAND ANY CANDLESTICK PATTERN WITHOUT MEMORIZING A SINGLE ONE

Are you feeling overwhelmed with the various candlestick patterns out there? Don't worry; you don't have to remember them all. Instead, let me share with you the top three things you need to know to read any candlestick pattern like a pro. Think of it as a cheat sheet for candlestick patterns. Here are the essentials:

- The color of the body of the candlestick tells you which side, buyers, or sellers, is in control of the market.
- The length of the wick (the lines extending from the body) represents price rejection, indicating where the market tried to go but failed to reach.
- The ratio of the body to the wick provides you with the complete story of the price action for that period.

Let me show you more…

THE COLOR OF THE BODY TELLS YOU WHO'S IN CONTROL

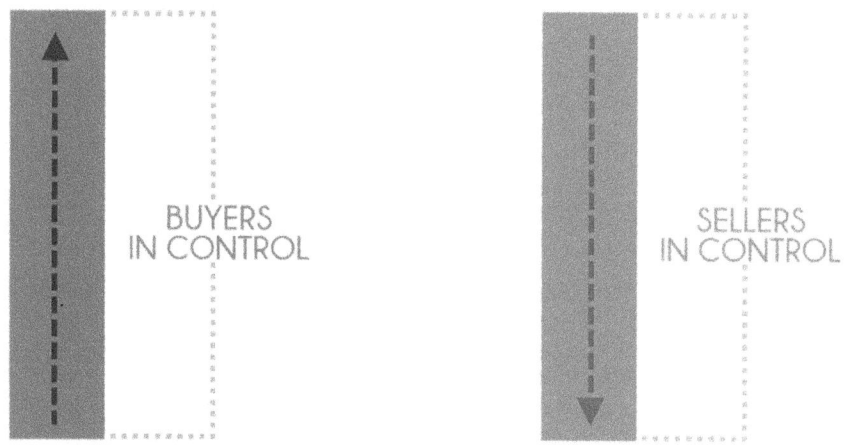

When you see a candle closing above the open, it's like a sign that the buyers are taking the reins, at least for the moment. It means that the market is closing higher than it opened, and that's generally a good thing for investors who are bullish on that stock.

On the other hand, if you see a candle closing below the open, it's like a signal that the sellers are dominating the market for now. This means that the market is closing lower than it opened, which is usually a cause for concern for investors who are long on that stock.

So, keep an eye on those candlestick charts and pay attention to whether the candles are closing above or below the open. It could give you some insight into which way the market is leaning at that moment.

THE LENGTH OF THE WICK REPRESENTS PRICE REJECTION

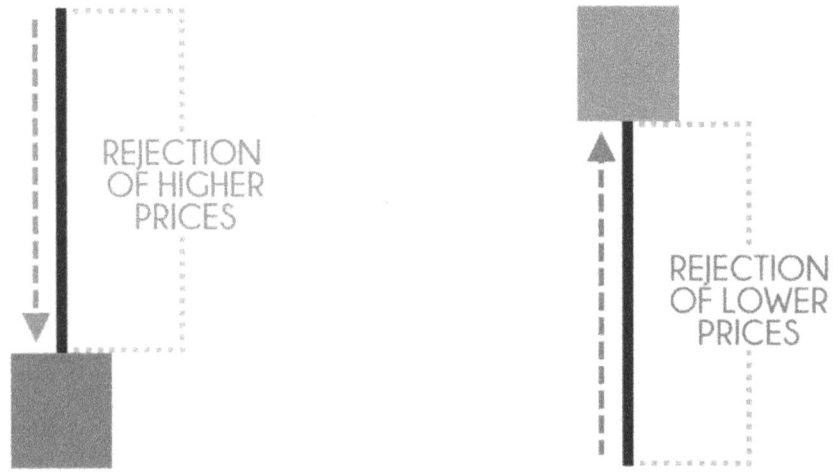

Let's talk about something that every trader should know - candlestick shadows, also known as wicks. They can give you a wealth of information about the market sentiment, so pay attention!

If you notice a long upper shadow, it's like the market is saying "Oh no, you don't!" to higher prices. It means that the buyers tried to push the price up, but the sellers were having none of it. Conversely, if you see a long lower shadow, it's like the market is saying "No way, Jose!" to lower prices. This indicates that the sellers tried to push the price down, but the buyers weren't having it.

But what if you see a short shadow? Well, that's like the market is saying "Meh" to the price action. It means that there was some resistance, but it wasn't very strong. Think of it like a half-hearted attempt to push the price up or down.

THE RATIO OF THE BODY TO THE WICK TELLS YOU THE "WHOLE STORY"

I'm about to drop some candlestick chart knowledge on you that'll have you feeling like a market expert in no time.

You see, when a candle has a long upper shadow, it's basically a big middle finger to higher prices. It means that buyers tried to push the price up, but the sellers were like, "Nah, we're not having it today." And when you get a long lower shadow, it's like the sellers are giving a big "hell no" to lower prices. They're saying, "We won't stand for this, and we're not selling at that price."

But what if the shadow is short, you ask? Well, that's when things get a little more nuanced. A short shadow means that there was only weak resistance to the price, either from buyers or sellers. It's like when you're trying to push a door open, and it's not locked, but it's still a bit heavy. It's not a complete block, but it's not exactly a free pass either.

So, the next time you're looking at a candlestick chart and you see those shadows, remember that they're telling you a story. And now you know what that story is, whether it's a big "hell no" to higher or lower prices, or just a bit of resistance that's not quite enough to stop the price from moving.

Here are a couple of examples...

Strong bullish close vs weak price rejection:

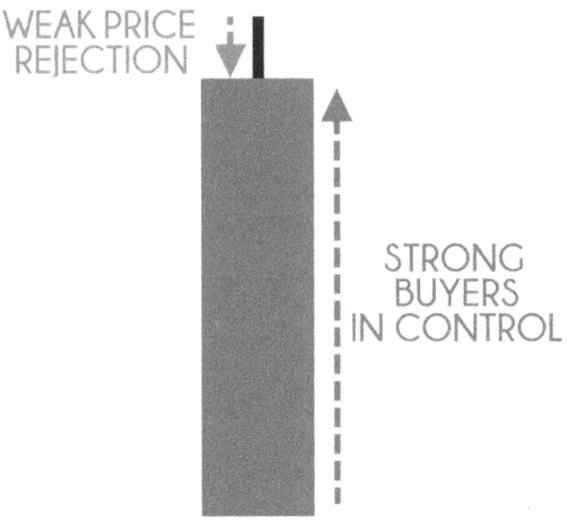

This tells you that the buyers are in control as there is minimal selling pressure (the short upper wick).

Strong price rejection vs weak bullish close:

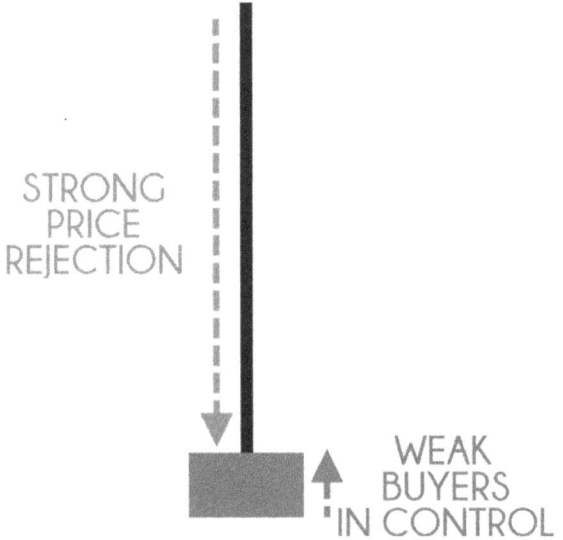

The sellers are in control as they have reversed most of the earlier gains (long upper shadow). So, even though it's a bullish close, the overall picture is bearish momentarily.

Does it make sense? Great!

Now you have what it takes to read any candlestick pattern without having to memorize a single one.

CHART PATTERNS

I hope that after learning about Candlestick patterns in the previous chapter, you have also practiced on the chart. Practicing will help you to become perfect.

Let's continue our journey and learn about different chart patterns that can help us make our daily targets a reality every day.

So, are you ready to take your trading skills to the next level? If so, then buckle up because we're about to dive into the exciting world of chart patterns!

Think of chart patterns as the body to candlestick patterns' soul. They're two sides of the same coin, and mastering both is key to becoming a successful trader. Chart patterns are a vital part of price action analysis, helping you identify the right trading trend and make profitable decisions. And who doesn't want to make a profit, right?

If you've been following along with our previous chapter on candlestick patterns, you've hopefully been practicing on real charts to perfect your skills. Now, it's time to expand your knowledge and take on the challenge of learning different chart patterns.

Why is it so important to learn chart patterns? Simply put, they can give you a major advantage in the markets. By analysing charts, you can identify patterns that signal the direction of price movements, allowing you to make informed trading decisions. This can help you time your trades more effectively, manage your risks, and improve your overall technical analysis skills.

But don't worry, learning chart patterns doesn't have to be dry and boring. In fact, it can be an exciting and rewarding experience! Imagine being able to read charts like a pro and confidently make profitable trades. With the right education and practice, this can be your reality.

So, let's dive in and explore various chart patterns together. We'll show you how to identify them, interpret their meanings, and use them to make real profits in the markets. Get ready to take your trading game to the next level!

HOW TO TRADE CHART PATTERN: SEGMENT 1

We always use the Trading with Tarun (TWT) formula to trade these chart patterns which is

1. 3 touches (of the trendline on either side)
2. Consolidation (before the breakdown or breakout)
3. Trade on Breakout / Breakdown

In the above example, we wait for a minimum of three touches to the trend line on either side and wait for the price to consolidate in small candles near the trendline before a breakout/breakdown occurs. We then take the trade accordingly.

Target: Whatever the difference between the 1st touch and 2nd touch (as shown in the picture) will be the target on either side.

Stop Loss: The SL will be the low of the breakout candle and the high of the breakdown candle, respectively.

SEGEMENT 1 CHART PATTERNS

ASCENDING BROADENING

In this pattern, the price movement widens over time as the highs and lows become increasingly spread out. Think of it like a tug-of-war between buyers and sellers, causing the price to swing back and forth within the expanding wedge. The upper trendline connects the higher highs, while the lower trendline connects the lower lows, creating a unique and recognizable wedge shape.

Now, don't be fooled by this pattern's indecisive nature. Ascending Broadening patterns can actually be a great way for traders to identify potential buying or selling opportunities. For example, if you see a breakout above the upper trendline, it could be a signal to buy. On the other hand, a breakdown below the lower trendline could be a signal to sell.

So, whether you're a seasoned trader or just starting out, keep an eye out for Ascending Broadening patterns in the charts. With the right knowledge and practice, you could be on your way to making profitable trades in no time!

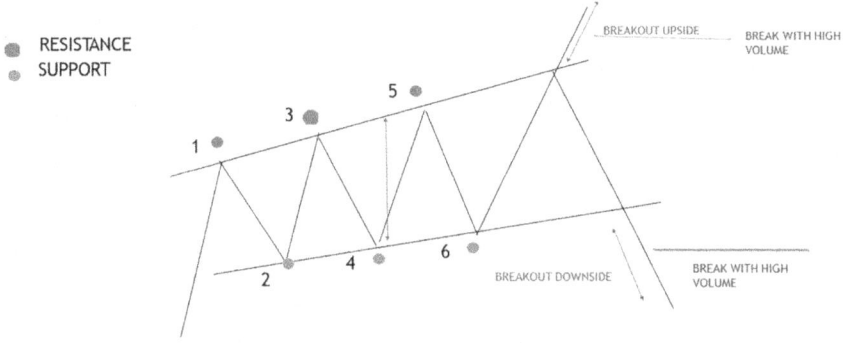

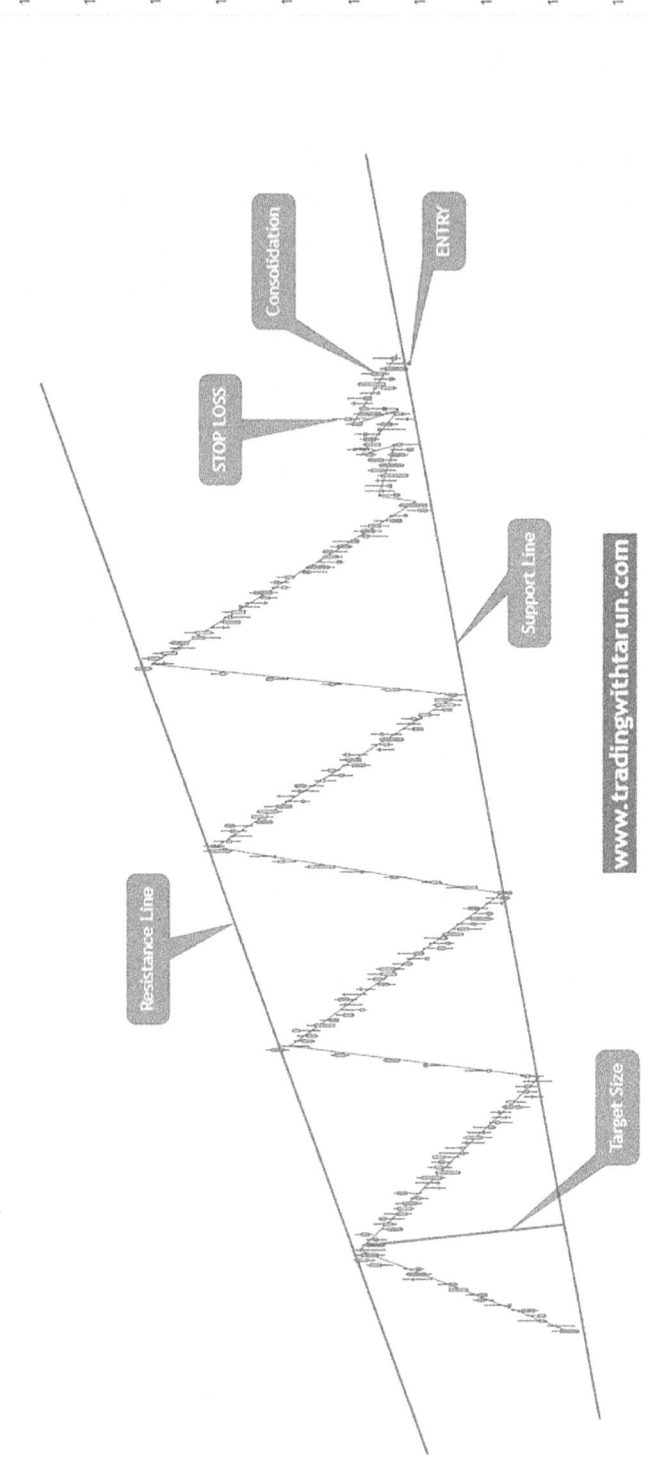

DESCENDING BROADENING

In this pattern, the price movement widens over time as the highs and lows become increasingly spread out. The upper trendline connects the lower highs, while the lower trendline connects the higher lows. These trendlines diverge from each other, creating the wedge shape, which is the opposite of the ascending broadening pattern.

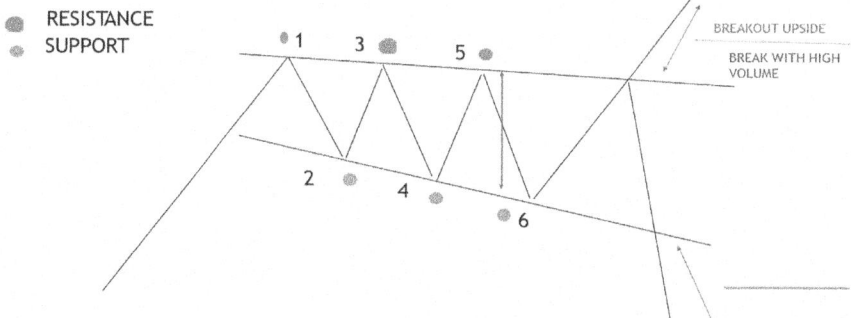

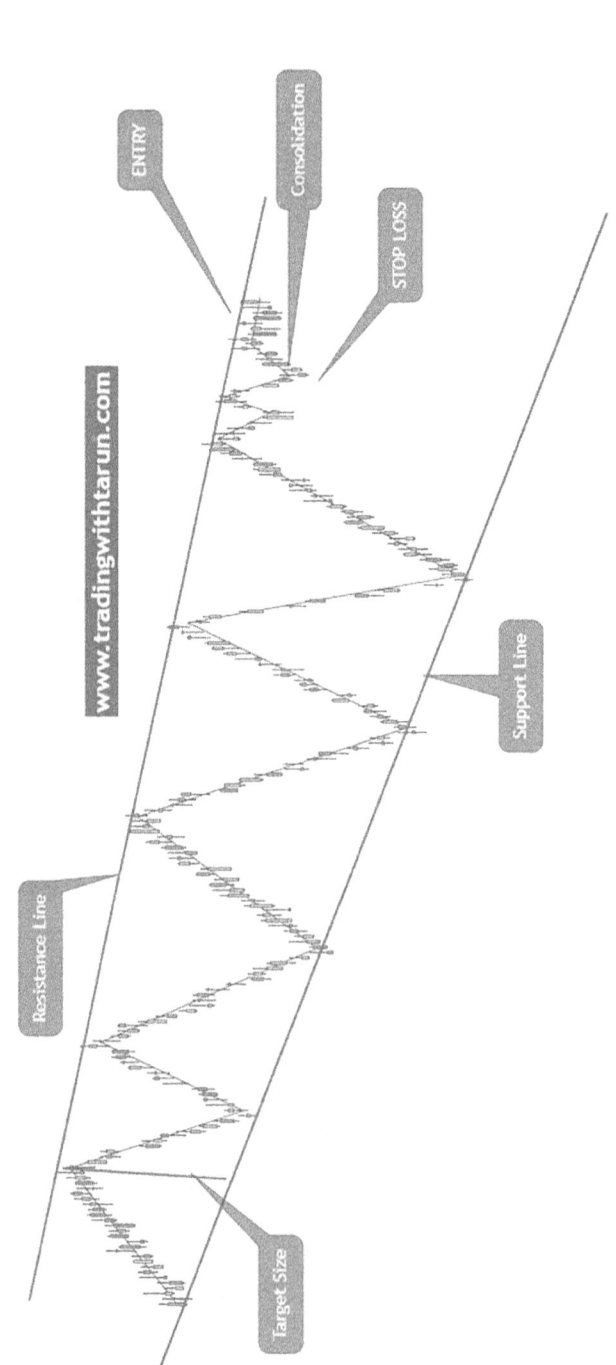

Traders may use Descending Broadening patterns to identify potential buying or selling opportunities, much like the Ascending Broadening pattern. They may look for a breakout above the upper trendline as a signal to buy, or a breakdown below the lower trendline as a signal to sell.

BULLISH CHANNEL (ASCENDING CHANNEL)

In this pattern, the price movement moves in an upward direction, but in a controlled and predictable manner, with the upper trendline connecting the higher highs and the lower trendline connecting the higher lows. The price tends to stay within the channel and bounces off the trendlines.

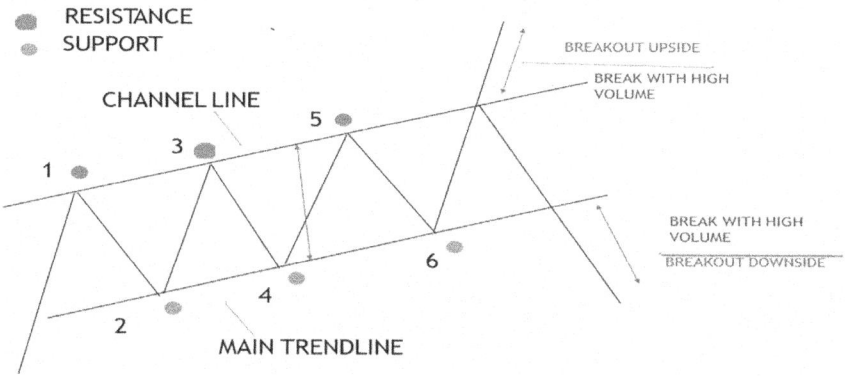

Bullish Channels are generally seen as a sign of a strong uptrend, with buyers dominating the market and pushing prices higher. Traders may use Bullish Channels to identify potential buying opportunities, looking for a bounce off the lower trendline as a signal to buy.

However, it is important to note that prices can break out of the Bullish Channel, signaling a potential trend reversal. Traders should always use the Bullish Channel in conjunction with other technical and fundamental analysis tools to make informed trading decisions.

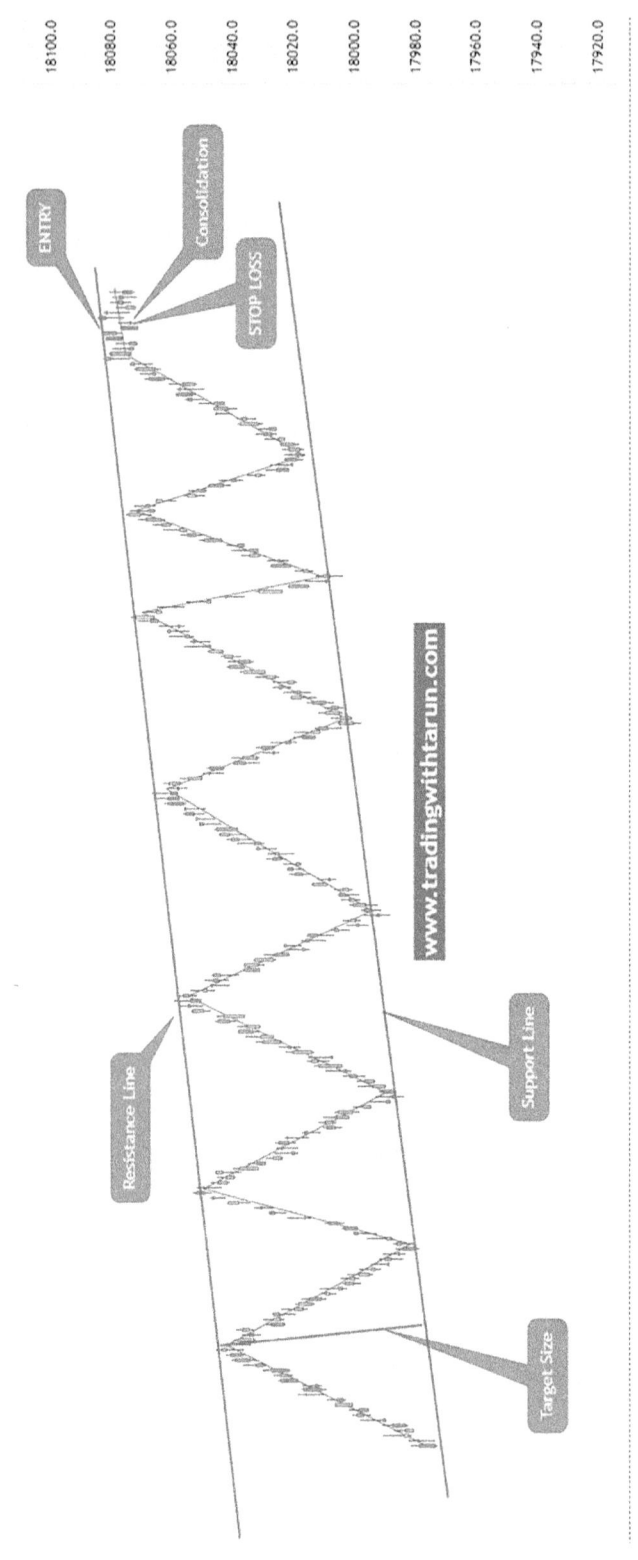

BEARISH CHANNEL (DESENDING CHANNEL)

In this pattern, the price movement moves in a downward direction, but in a controlled and predictable manner, with the upper trendline connecting the lower highs and the lower trendline connecting the lower lows. The price tends to stay within the channel and bounces off the trendlines.

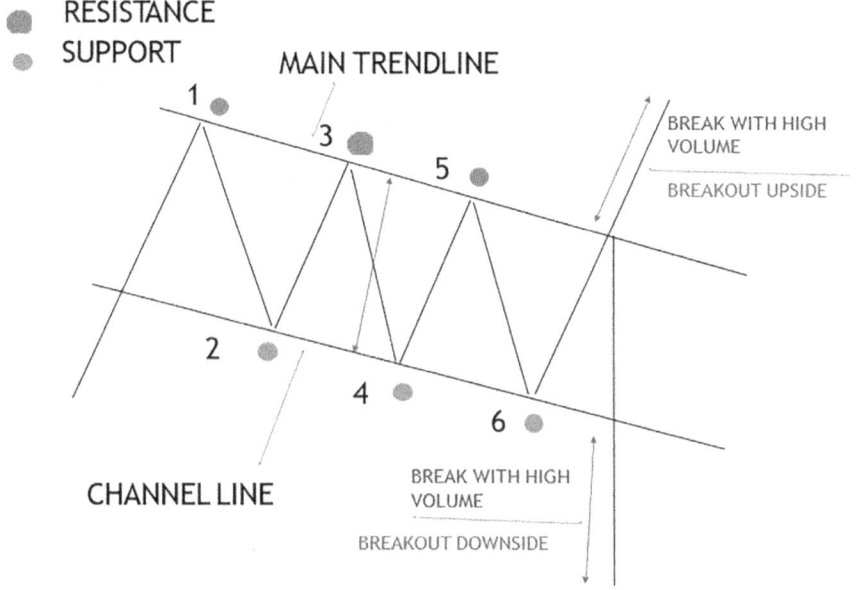

Bearish Channels are generally seen as a sign of a strong downtrend, with sellers dominating the market and pushing prices lower. Traders may use Bearish Channels to identify potential selling opportunities, looking for a bounce off the upper trendline as a signal to sell.

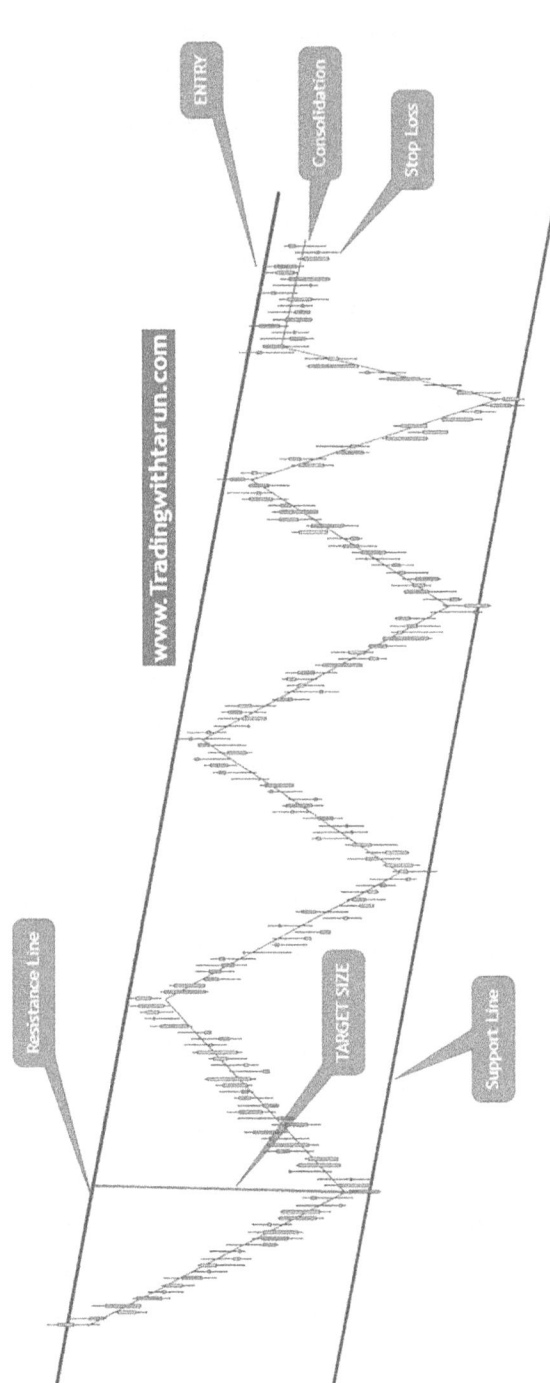

EQUAL CHANNEL (PARALLEL CHANNEL)

In this pattern, the price movement moves neither upward nor downward but rather in a stable, sideways manner. The upper trendline connects the highs, while the lower trendline connects the lows, and both trendlines are parallel to each other.

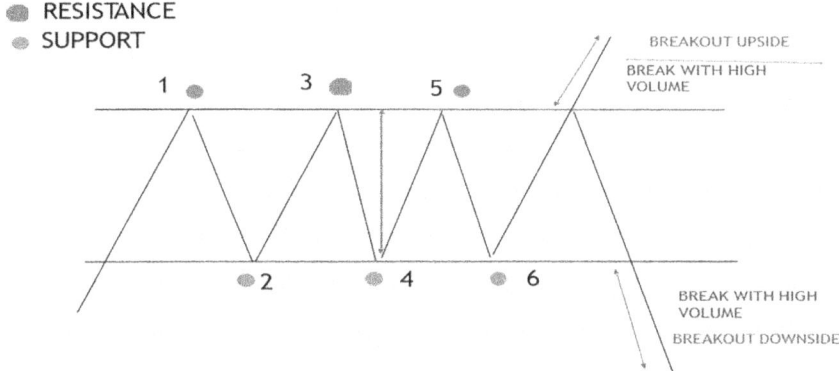

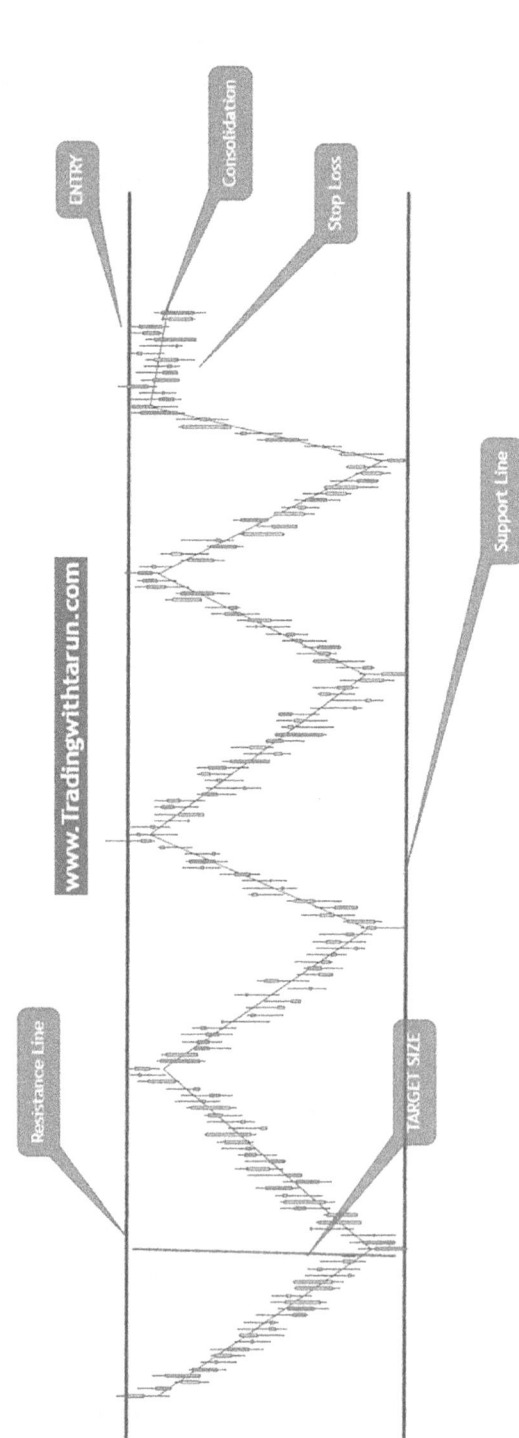

FALLING WEDGE

In this pattern, the price movement moves in a downward direction, but the rate of decline slows down over time, creating a wedge shape. The lower trendline connects the lower lows, while the upper trendline connects the lower highs. As the pattern progresses, the price tends to move towards the apex of the wedge.

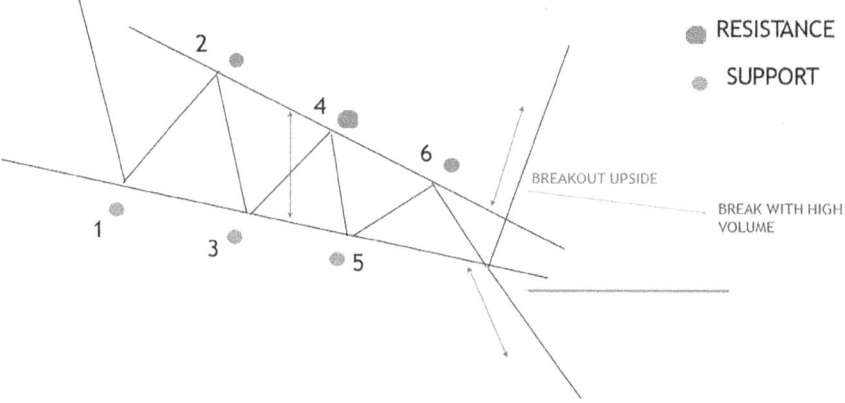

Falling Wedges are generally seen as a sign of a potential trend reversal, with prices moving from a downtrend to an uptrend. Traders may use Falling Wedges to identify potential buying opportunities, looking for a breakout above the upper trendline as a signal to buy.

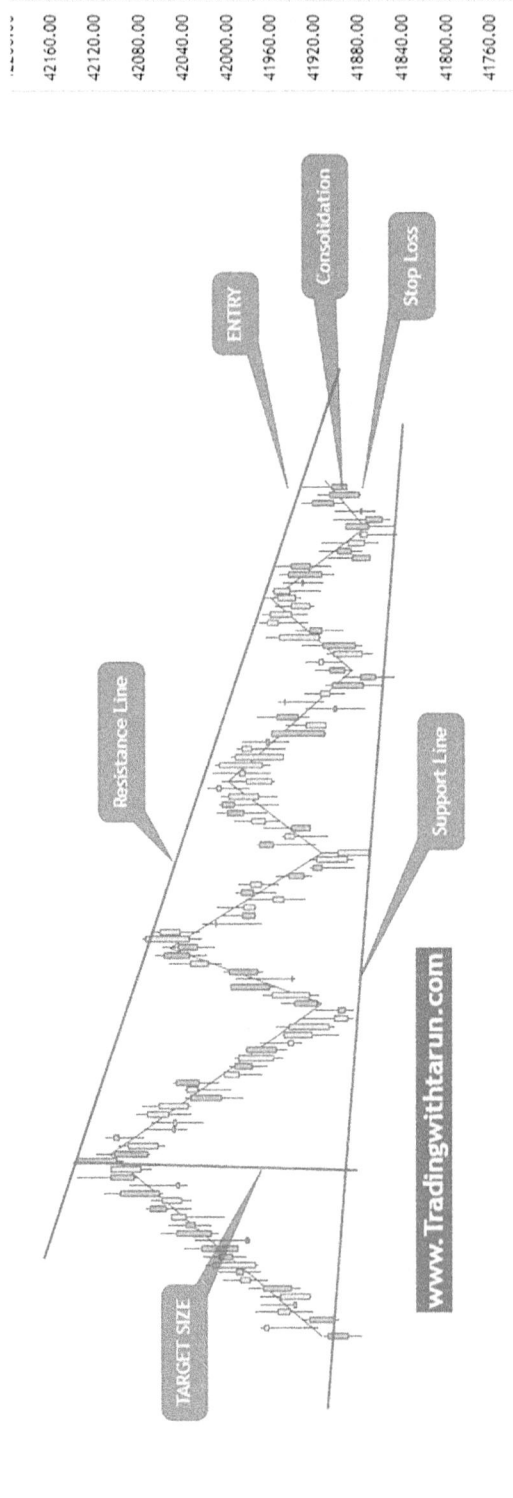

RISING WEDGE

In this pattern, the price movement moves in an upward direction, but the rate of ascent slows down over time, creating the wedge shape. The upper trendline connects the higher highs, while the lower trendline connects the higher lows. As the pattern progresses, the price tends to move towards the apex of the wedge.

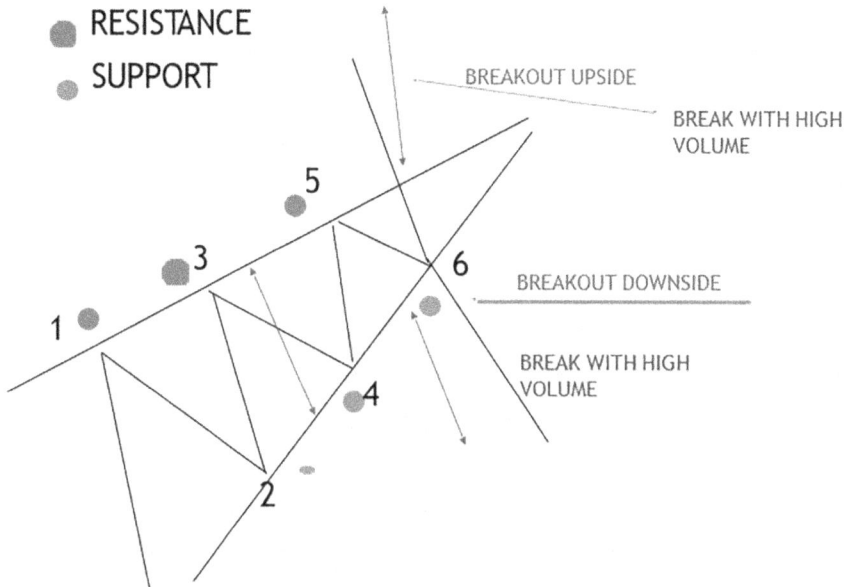

Rising Wedges are generally seen as a sign of a potential trend reversal, with prices moving from an uptrend to a downtrend. Traders may use Rising Wedges to identify potential selling opportunities, looking for a breakout below the lower trendline as a signal to sell.

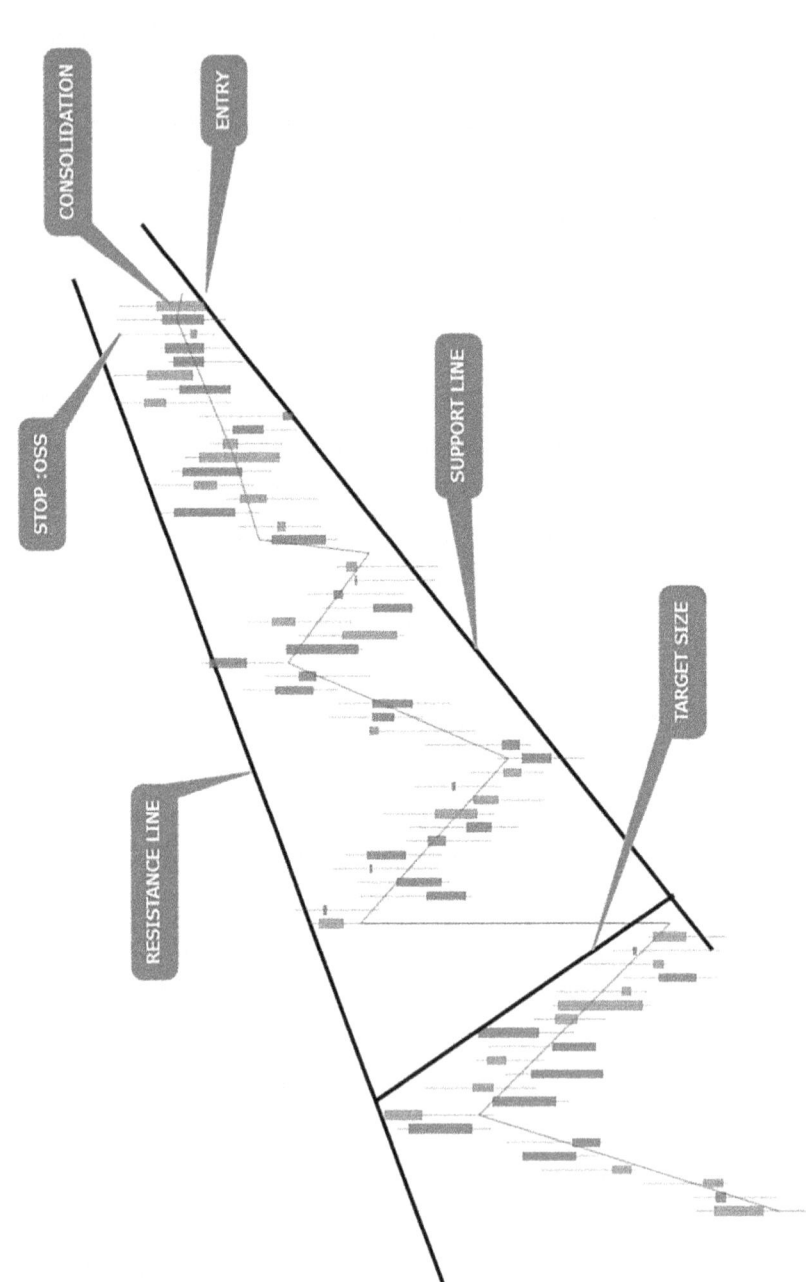

SYMMETRICAL TRIANGLE

In this pattern, the upper trendline connects the series of lower highs, while the lower trendline connects the series of higher lows. As the pattern progresses, the price tends to move towards the apex of the triangle, where the upper and lower trendlines converge.

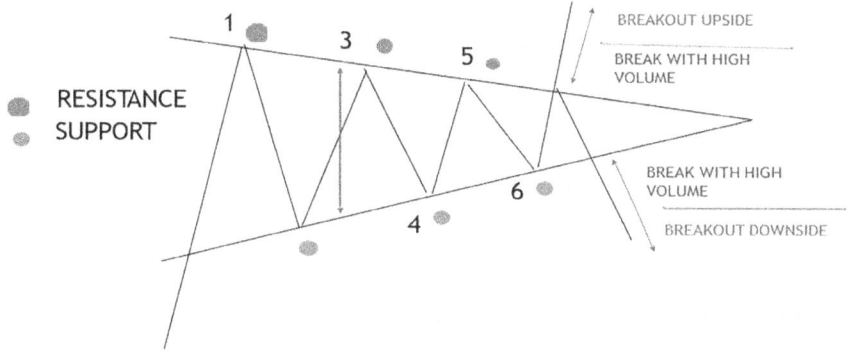

The Symmetrical Triangle pattern can be interpreted in different ways depending on the context of the market. It can be a continuation pattern, where the price movement continues in the same direction after the triangle is broken. Alternatively, it can also be a reversal pattern, where the price movement reverses direction after the triangle is broken.

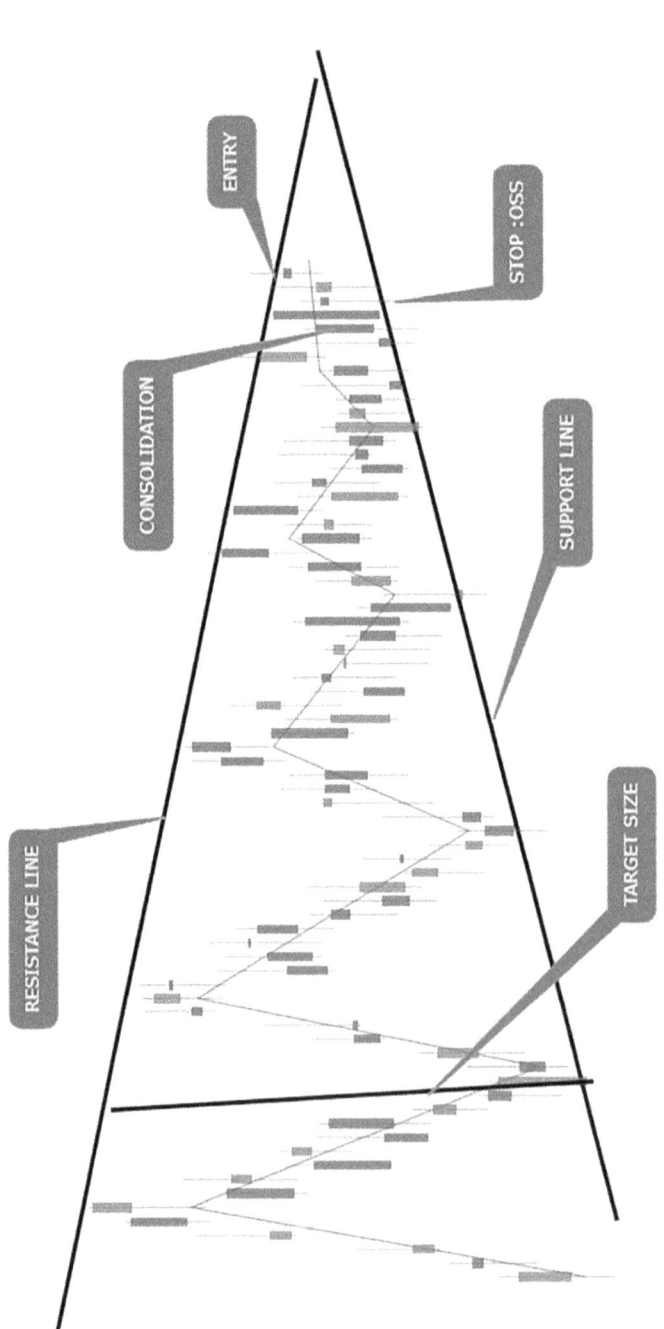

ASCENDING TRIANGLE

In this pattern, the upper trendline is flat and connects the series of highs, while the lower trendline is rising and connects the series of higher lows. As the pattern progresses, the price tends to move towards the flat upper trendline, where it may encounter resistance.

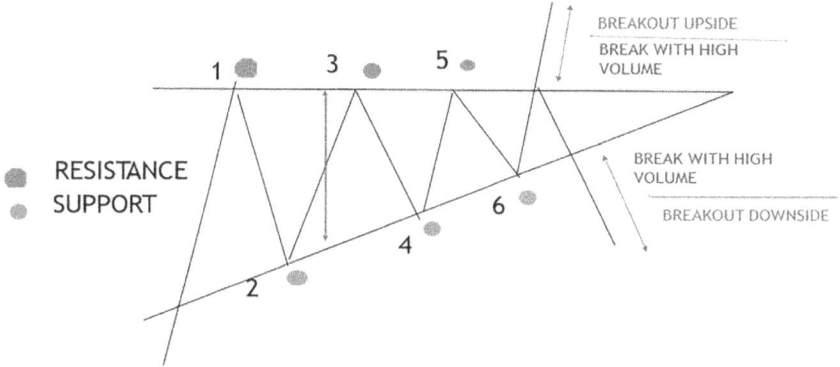

The Ascending Triangle pattern is typically considered a continuation pattern, where the price movement continues in the same upward direction after the triangle is broken above the flat upper trendline. Traders may use the Ascending Triangle pattern to identify potential buying opportunities, looking for a breakout above the upper trendline as a signal to buy.

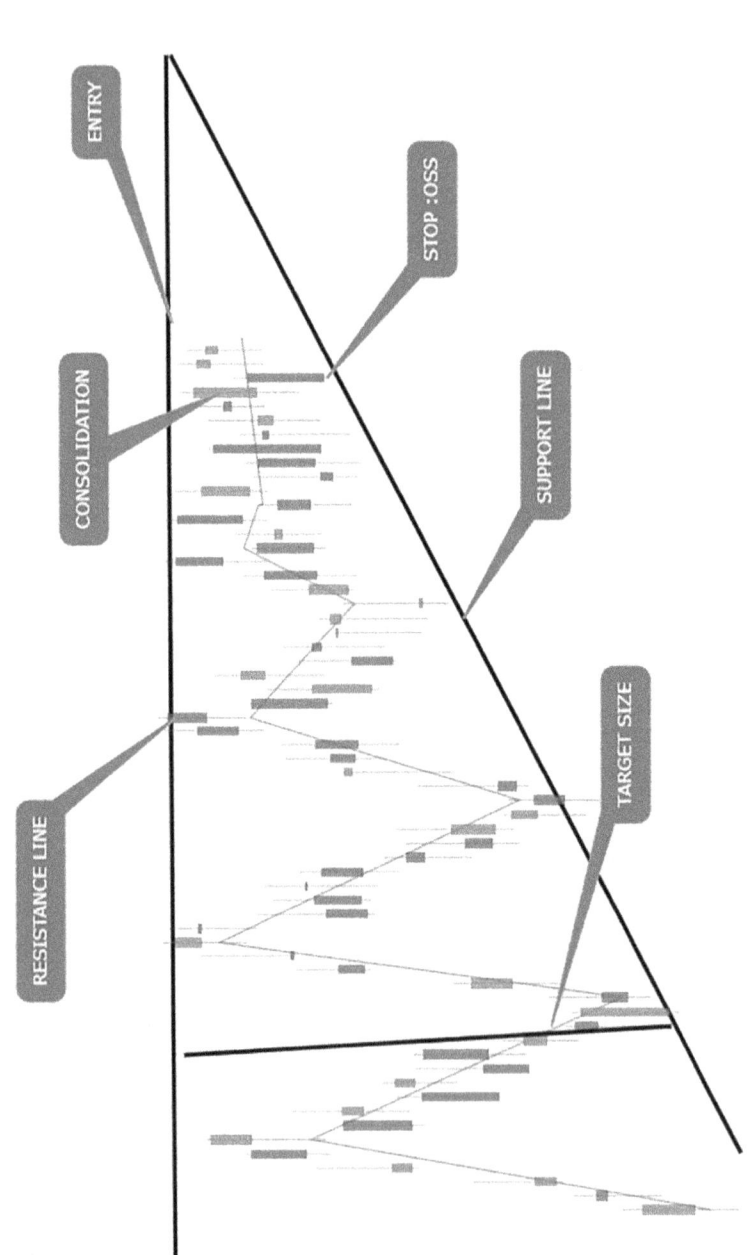

DESCENDING TRIANGLE

The Descending Triangle is a technical analysis pattern that traders use to identify potential selling opportunities in financial markets. Picture a triangle with a flat lower trendline and a declining upper trendline - that's the Descending Triangle!

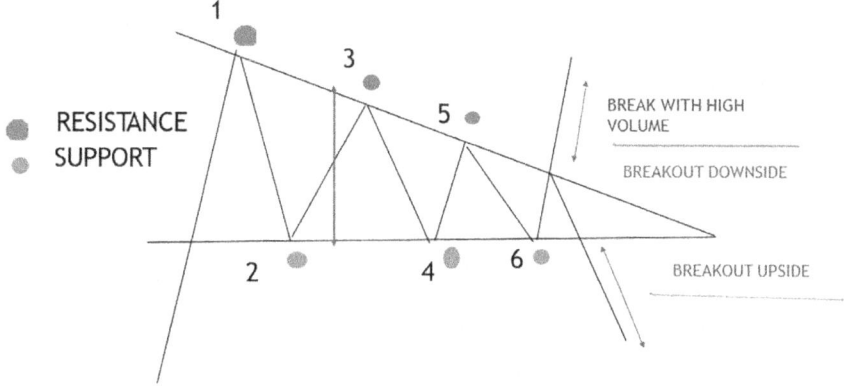

As the pattern progresses, the price movement tends to approach the flat lower trendline, where it may find support. But if the support level is broken, it can signal a prime opportunity for traders to sell at a higher price before the price movement continues its downward trend.

The Descending Triangle is a continuation pattern, which means that the price movement is likely to continue in the same downward direction after the triangle is broken below the lower trendline. This is a valuable insight for traders who are looking to make informed selling decisions.

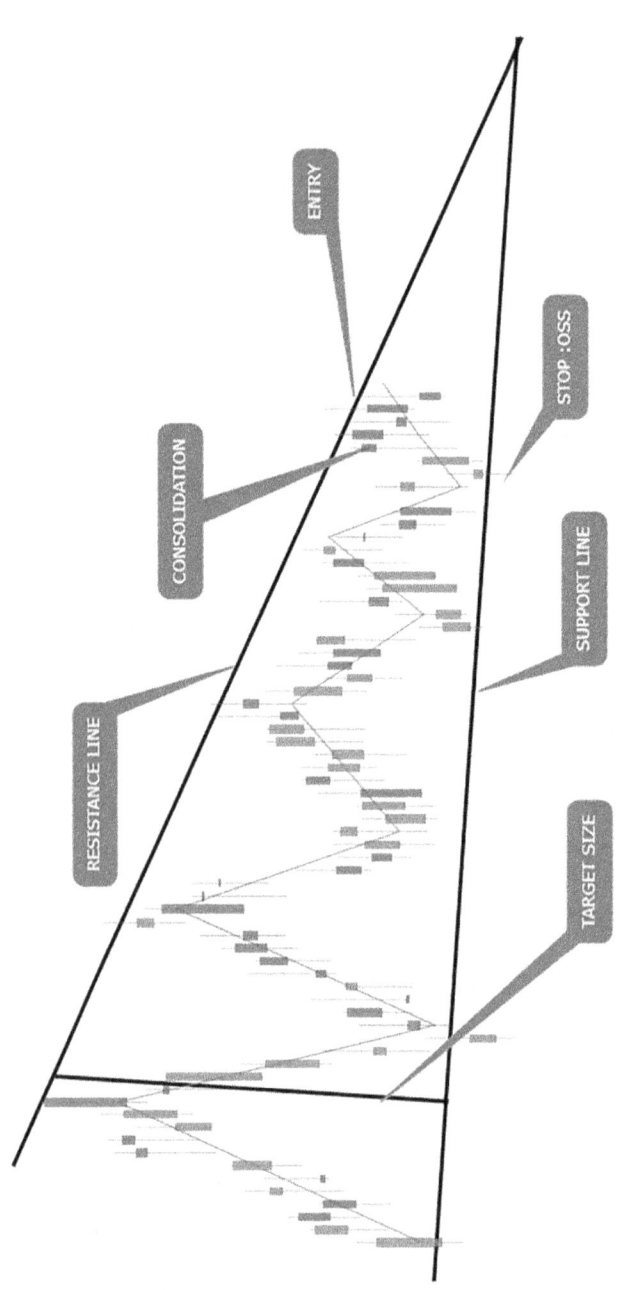

DOUBLE TOP

Imagine you're playing a game of tug-of-war, and your team pulls hard to get the rope to a certain point. You manage to get it there, but the other team pulls back and stops you from moving any further. You try again and manage to get the rope to that same point, but once again, the other team pulls back and stops you from advancing. This is what the Double Top pattern looks like!

The Double Top pattern is a powerful tool that traders use to identify potential trend reversals. It occurs when the price of an asset hits a resistance level twice and fails to break through it both times. The pattern looks like two peaks that are roughly equal in height, with a trough in between them.

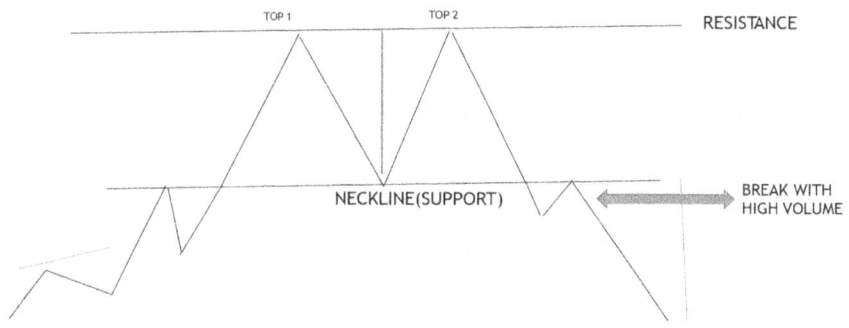

When this pattern appears, it is usually a sign that the upward trend is losing steam and a downward trend may be on the horizon. Traders who spot this pattern can use it to their advantage by selling at a higher price before the price movement continues its downward trend.

RESISTANCE LINE
TOP 1
TOP 2
TARGET SIZE
STOP :OSS
CONSOLIDATION
NECKLINE
SUPPORT LINE
ENTRY
42750.00
42500.00
42250.00
42000.00
41750.00
41500.00
41250.00
41000.00
40750.00
40500.00
40250.00
40000.00
39750.00
39500.00
39250.00
39000.00
38750.00

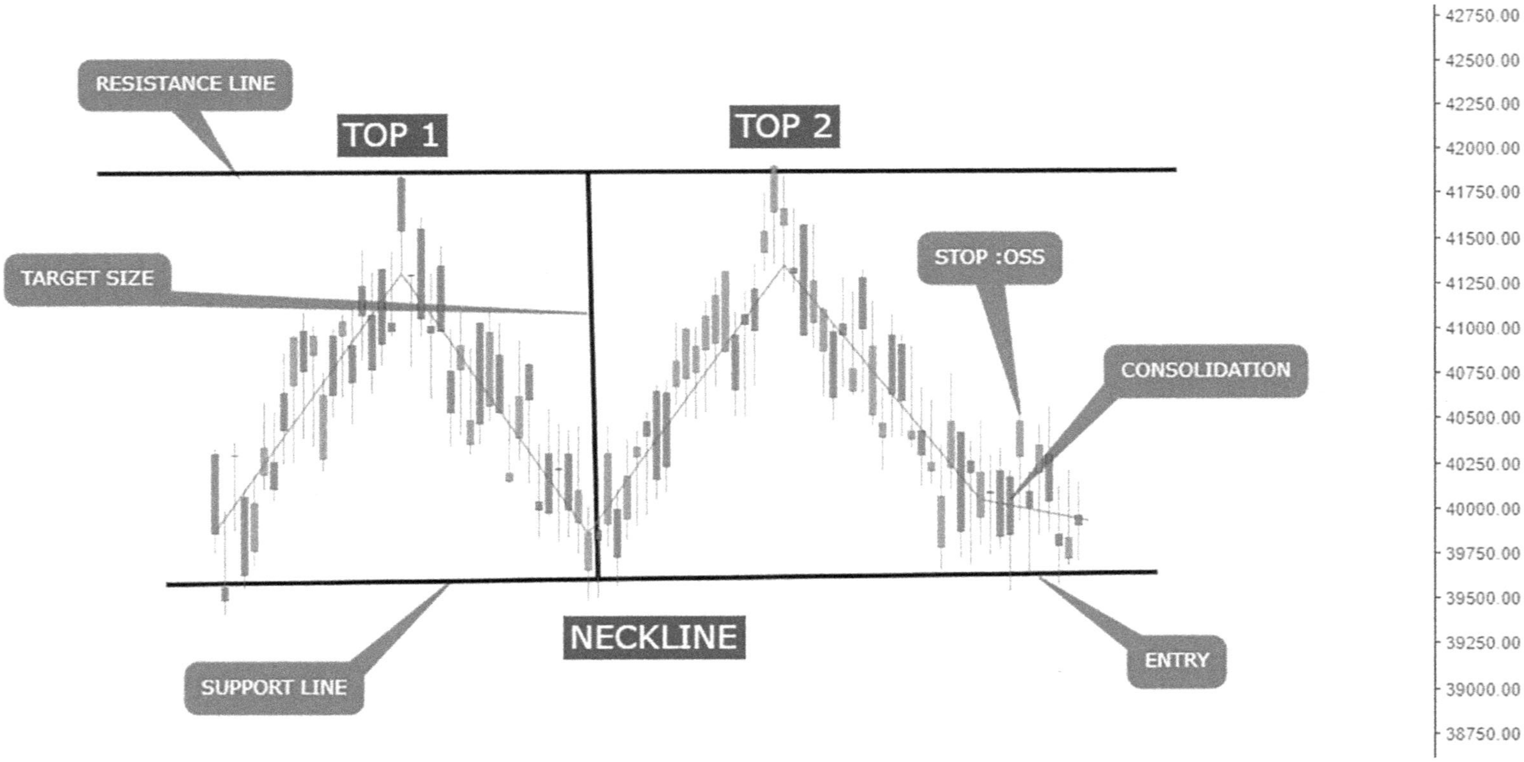

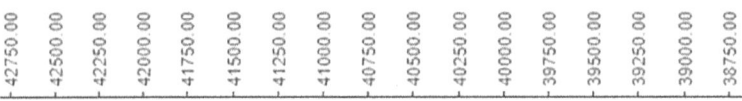

DOUBLE BOTTOM

Imagine you're hiking up a mountain and you come across a steep, rocky section. You slip and slide down to a certain point, but then you manage to regain your footing and climb back up. Unfortunately, you slip and fall again, but this time, you once again manage to regain your footing and climb back up to that same point. This is what the Double Bottom pattern looks like!

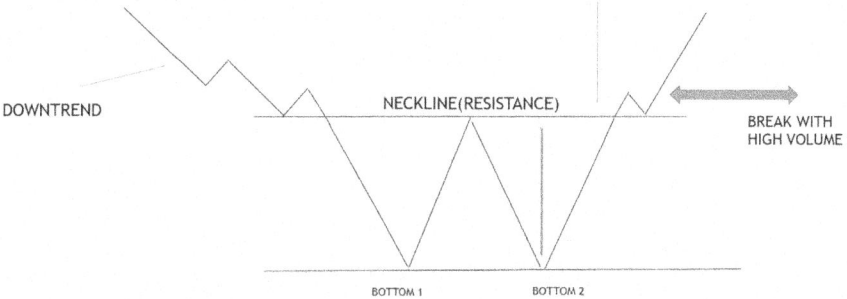

The Double Bottom pattern is a powerful tool that traders use to identify potential trend reversals. It is the inverse of the Double Top pattern, occurring when the price of an asset hits a support level twice and bounces back up each time. The pattern looks like two troughs that are roughly equal in depth, with a peak in between them.

When this pattern appears, it is usually a sign that the downward trend is losing steam and an upward trend may be on the horizon. Traders who spot this pattern can use it to their advantage by buying at a lower price before the price movement continues its upward trend.

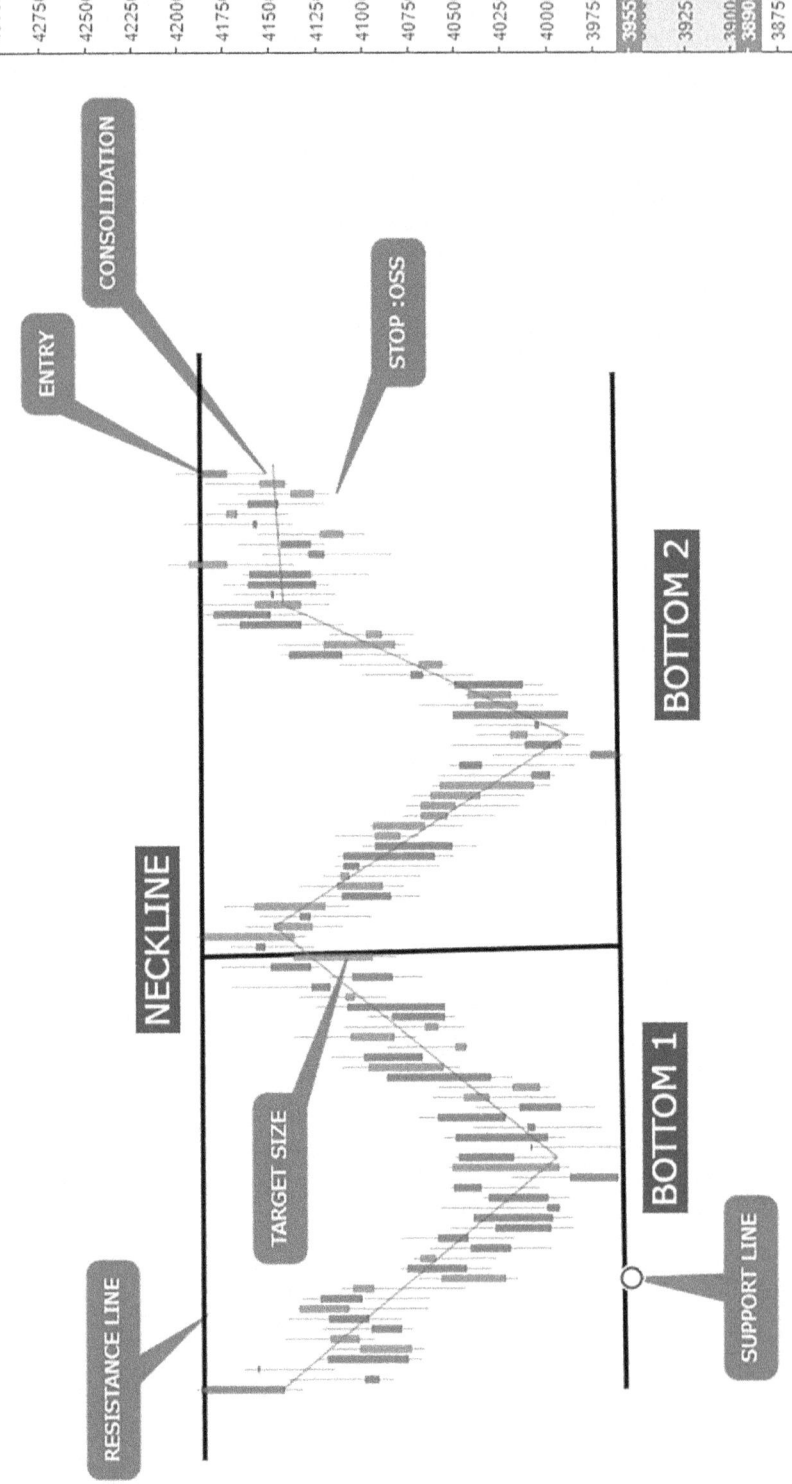

SEGMENT 2: CHART PATTERNS

Segment 2 is a set of special chart patterns which give the maximum returns, as per my understanding. The way we trade these chart patterns is different from Segment 1 chart patterns.

BEARISH FLAG

In this pattern, the price movement experiences a sharp decline, followed by a brief consolidation period where the price moves in a horizontal direction, forming a rectangular shape. The consolidation period represents a period of uncertainty in the market, where buyers and sellers are assessing the situation.

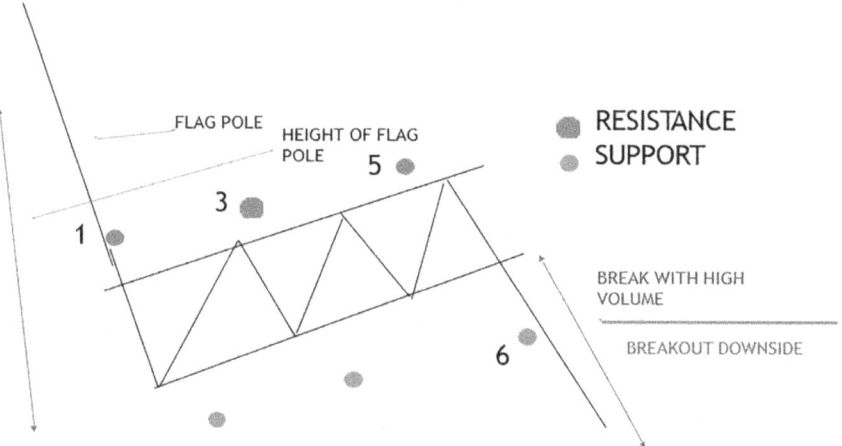

After the consolidation period, the price typically continues to move in a downward direction with the same intensity as before the consolidation period. The Bearish Flag pattern is called "bearish" because it indicates a continuation of a downward price trend.

Traders may use the Bearish Flag to identify potential selling opportunities, looking for a breakout below the lower trendline of the consolidation period as a signal to sell. However, it's important to use the Bearish Flag in conjunction with other technical and fundamental analysis tools to make informed trading decisions.

How to trade: The Bearish Flag is a 100% bearish chart pattern, hence we will be taking a bearish trade.

Entry: Take entry only when the lower bottom trendline is broken with good volume and the candle is closed below the trendline.

Target: The size of the pole from the top till the flag will be your target downside.

Stop Loss: The high of the range will be the stop loss on a closing basis.

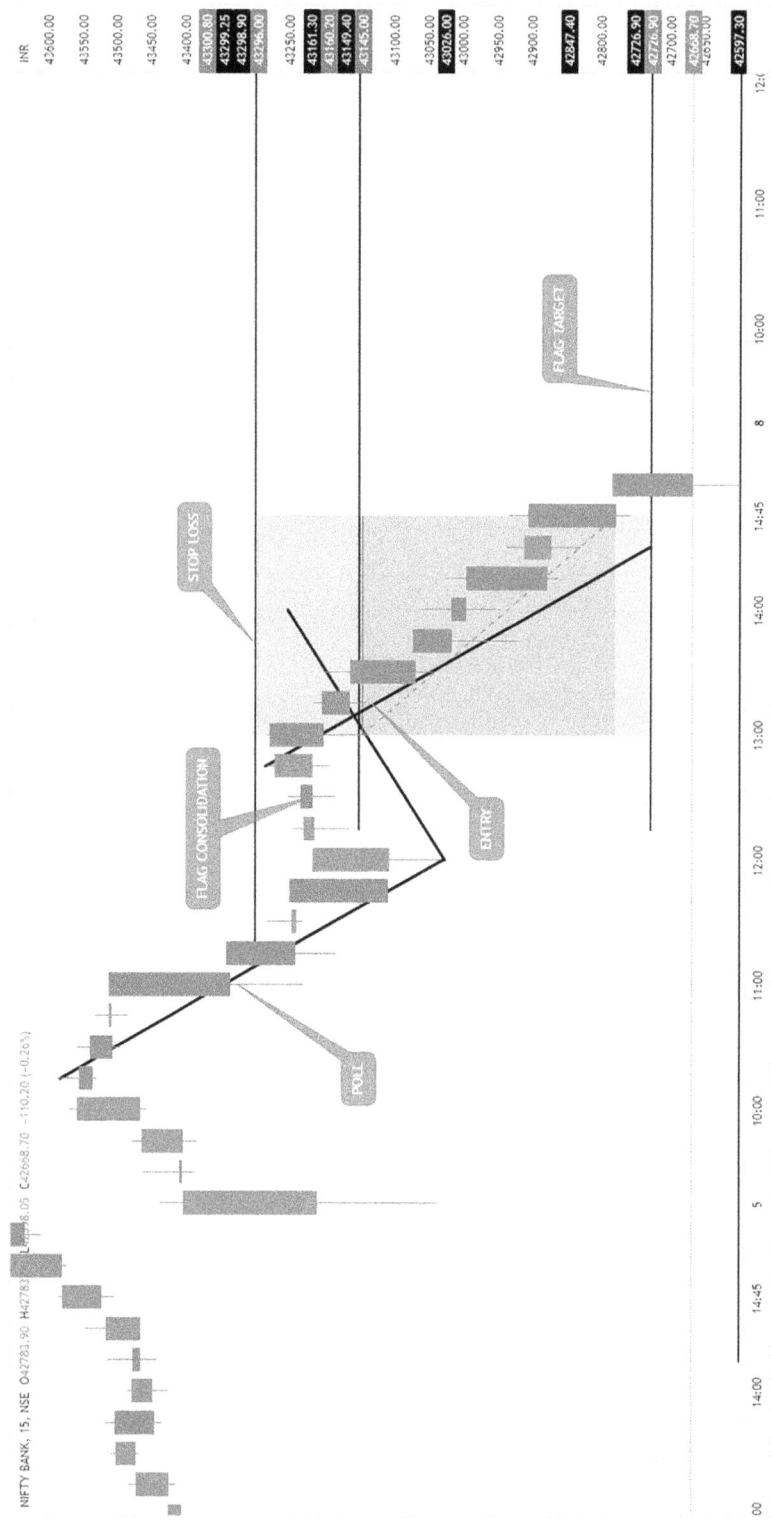

BULLISH FLAG

In this pattern, the price movement experiences a sharp increase, followed by a brief consolidation period where the price moves in a horizontal direction, forming a rectangular shape. The consolidation period represents a period of uncertainty in the market, where buyers and sellers are assessing the situation.

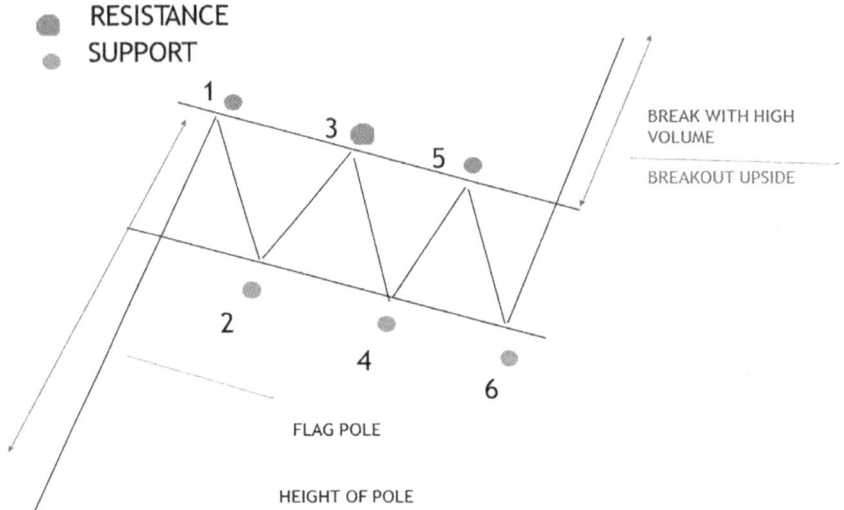

After the consolidation period, the price typically continues to move in an upward direction with the same intensity as before the consolidation period. The Bullish Flag pattern is called "bullish" because it indicates a continuation of an upward price trend.

How to trade: A Bullish Flag is a 100% Bullish Chart pattern, hence we will only be taking Bullish trades.

Entry: Take entry only when the upper trendline on consolidation is broken with good volume and the candle is closed above the trendline.

Target: The size of the pole from the till the flag will be your target upside.

Stop Loss: The low of the range will be the stop loss on a closing basis.

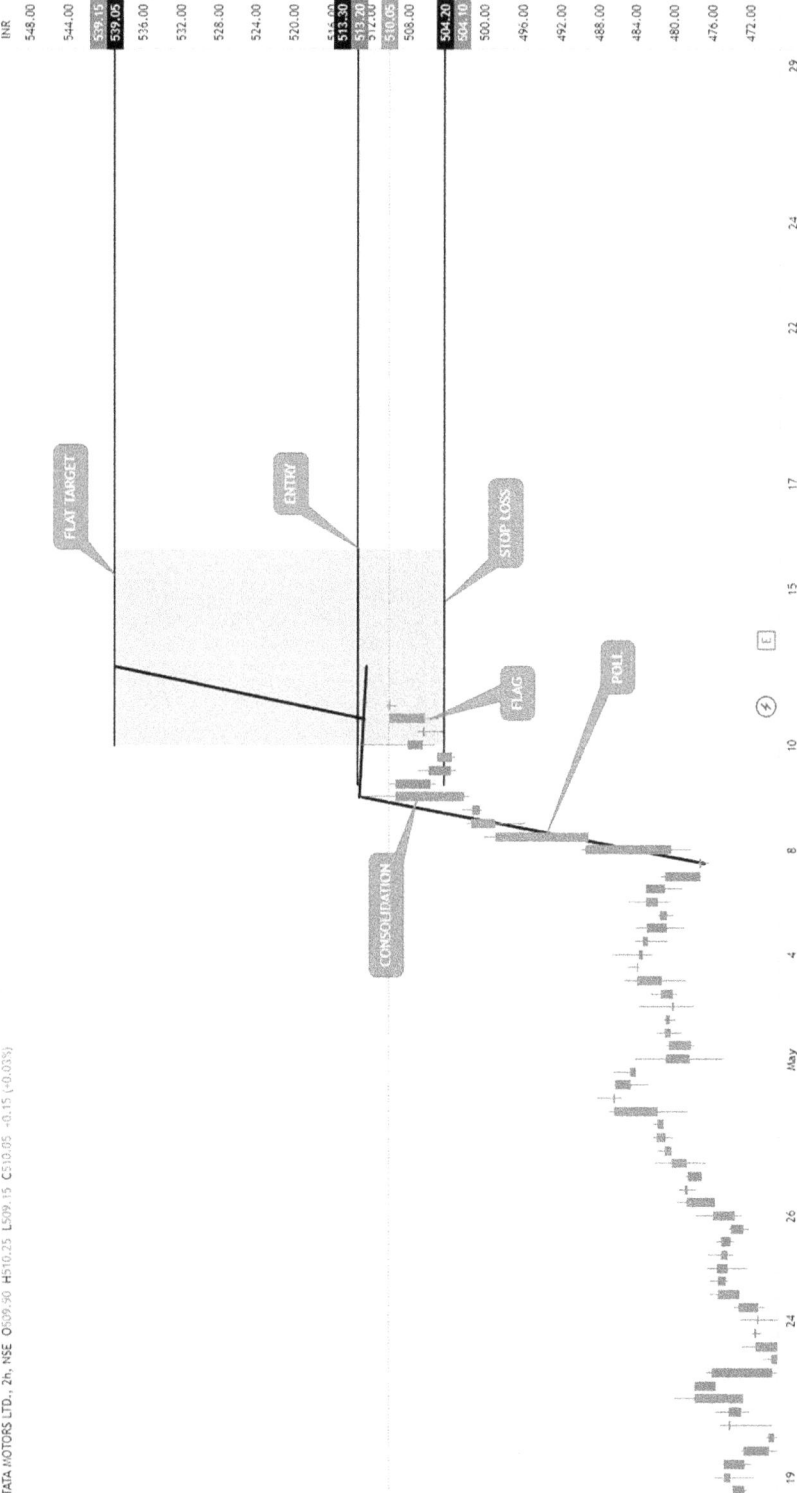

HEAD & SHOULDER

Imagine you're hiking in the mountains, and you come across a peak with two smaller peaks on either side. The middle peak is taller than the other two, and it looks like a head - that's the Head and Shoulders pattern!

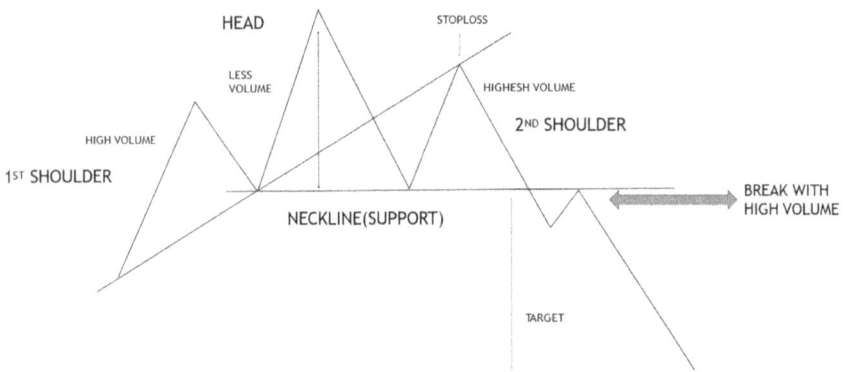

In the financial markets, the Head and Shoulders pattern is a technical analysis tool that traders use to identify potential trend reversals. The pattern consists of three peaks, with the middle peak being higher than the other two, which resemble shoulders. The left shoulder forms the first peak, followed by a pullback in price. The second peak, or the head, forms when the price rises higher than the left shoulder before falling back again. The right shoulder forms the third peak, which is typically lower than the head, before a final pullback in price.

When this pattern appears, it is usually a sign that the upward trend is about to end, and a downward trend may be on the horizon. Traders who spot this pattern can use it to their advantage by selling their shares at a higher price before the price movement drops.

How to Trade:

Entry: There are two ways of trading the Head & Shoulders.
1. Take entry once the neckline is broken upside.
2. Wait for the price to retest the neckline and enter into the trade.

Target: The size of the head (middle triangle) from bottom to top is the target upside.

SL: The low of the right shoulder will be the stop loss for the trade.

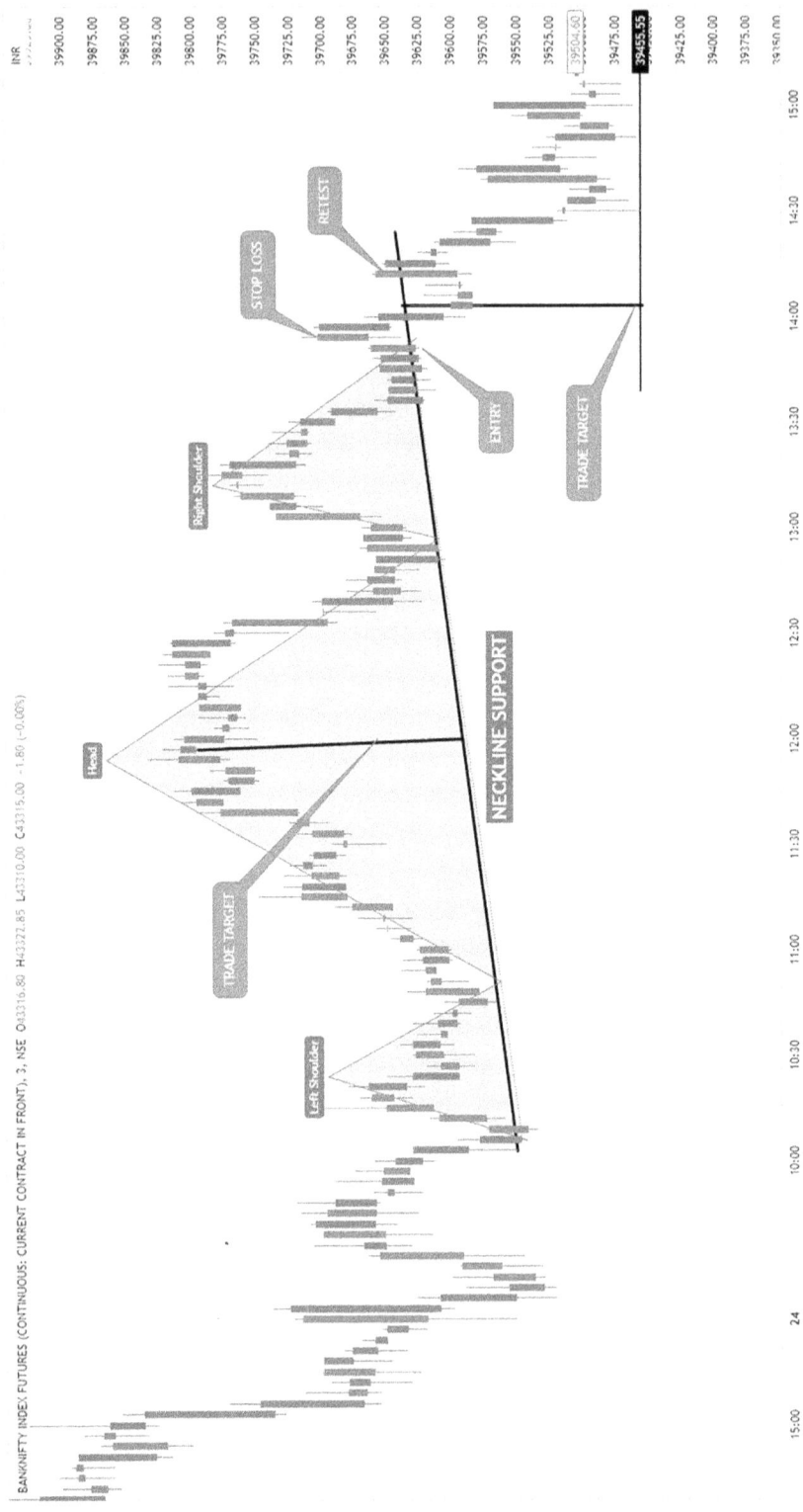

INVERTED HEAD & SHOULDER

Imagine you're on a roller coaster ride, and you go down a steep slope, only to come back up again and then go down another slope, before coming back up once more. That's what the Inverted Head and Shoulders pattern looks like!

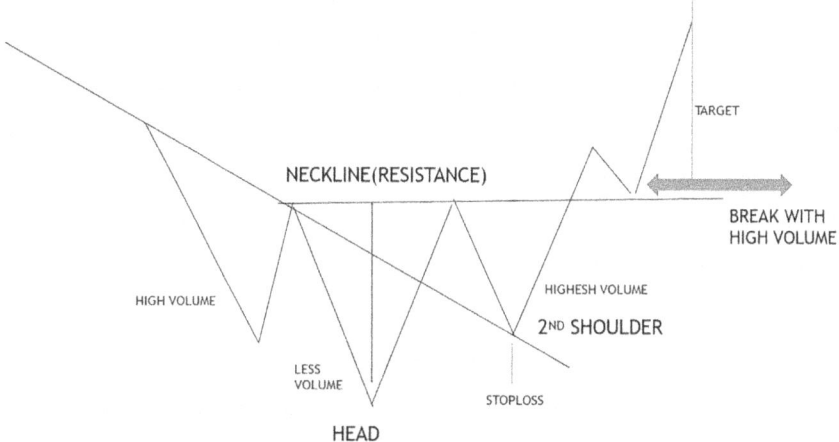

The inverted Head and Shoulders pattern is a powerful tool that traders use to identify potential trend reversals. It is the opposite of the regular Head and Shoulders pattern and consists of three troughs, with the middle trough (the "head") being lower than the two surrounding troughs (the "shoulders"). The left shoulder forms the first trough, followed by a rise in price. The head forms when the price falls below the left shoulder and then rises again to a level higher than the left shoulder. The right shoulder forms the third trough, which is typically higher than the head, followed by another rise in price.

When this pattern appears, it's usually a sign that the downward trend is coming to an end, and an upward trend may be on the horizon. Traders who spot this pattern can use it to their advantage by buying at a lower price before the price movement continues its upward trend.

How to Trade:

Entry: There are two ways of trading the Inverted Head & Shoulders.

1. Take entry once neckline is broken downside.
2. Wait for the price to retest the neckline and enter into the trade.

Target: The size of the head (middle triangle) from top to bottom is the target downside.

SL: The high of the right shoulder will be the stop loss for the trade.

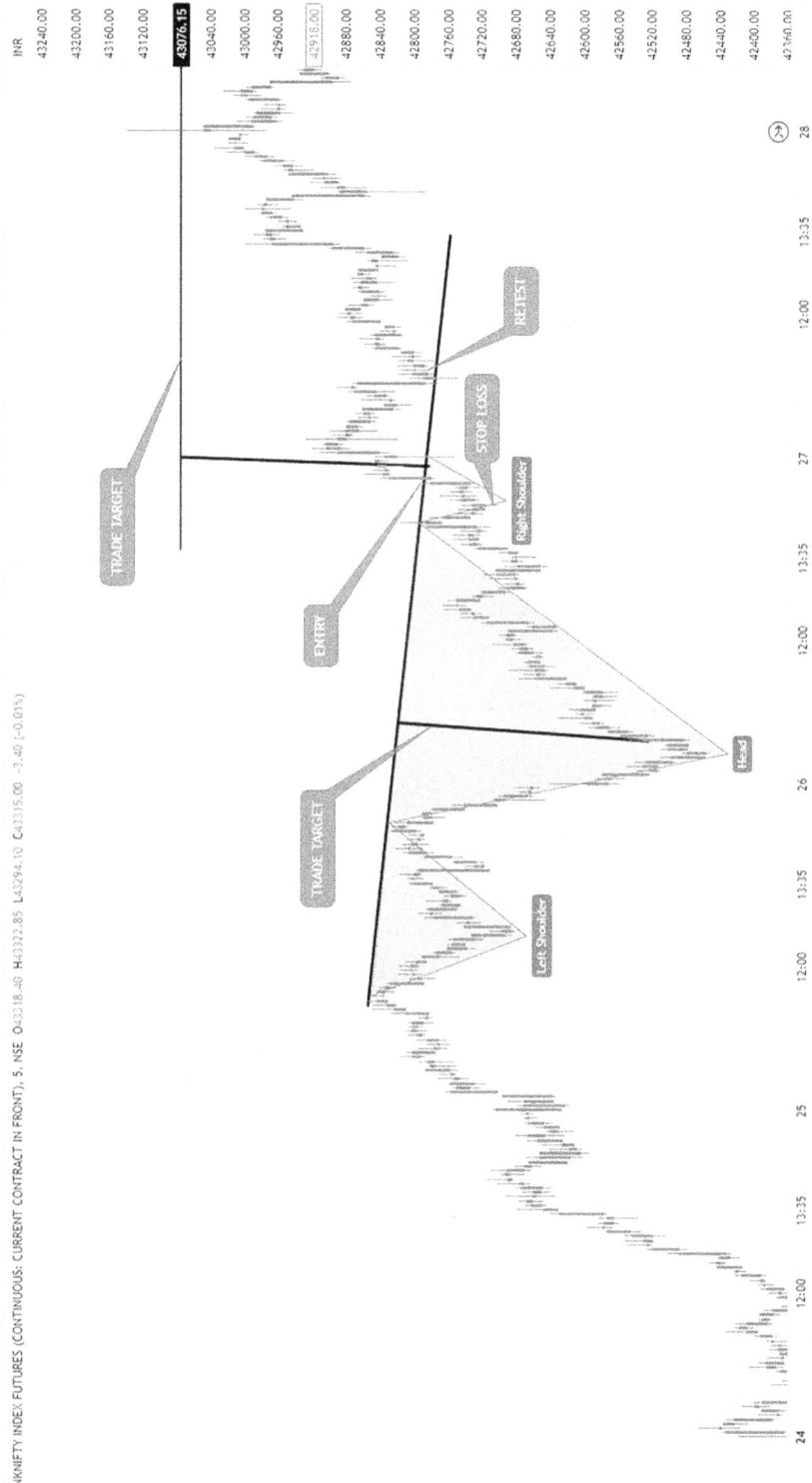

CUP WITH HANDLE

Imagine you're sitting in your kitchen, sipping a cup of coffee. As you set your cup down, you notice that it has a unique shape - it looks like a rounded cup with a small handle on the side. Little did you know, this cup shape could actually be a powerful tool for traders in financial markets!

The Cup with Handle pattern is a popular technical analysis tool used by traders to identify potential buying opportunities. The pattern is named for its distinctive shape, which resembles a cup with a handle. It typically starts with a gradual downward trend, forming the rounded bottom of the cup. The price then starts to rise again, forming the left side of the handle. The handle itself is formed by a short period of consolidation, with the price trading sideways in a tight range. Finally, the price breaks out above the handle, completing the pattern and signaling a potential bullish trend.

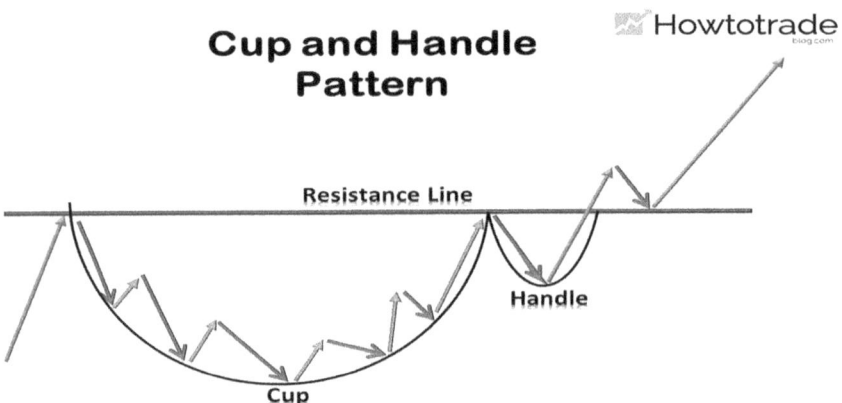

When traders spot this pattern, they may look to enter a long position, buying the asset in the hopes that the price will continue to rise. However, it's important to note that not every Cup with Handle pattern will lead to a profitable trade, and traders should always use other indicators and analysis tools to confirm the validity of the pattern.

How to trade:

Entry: Wait for the price to break the trendline after good consolidation and with good volume.

Target: The depth of the CUP will be targeted upside from the trendline.

SL: The low of the handle on the right will be the stop loss on a closing basis in the same time frame.

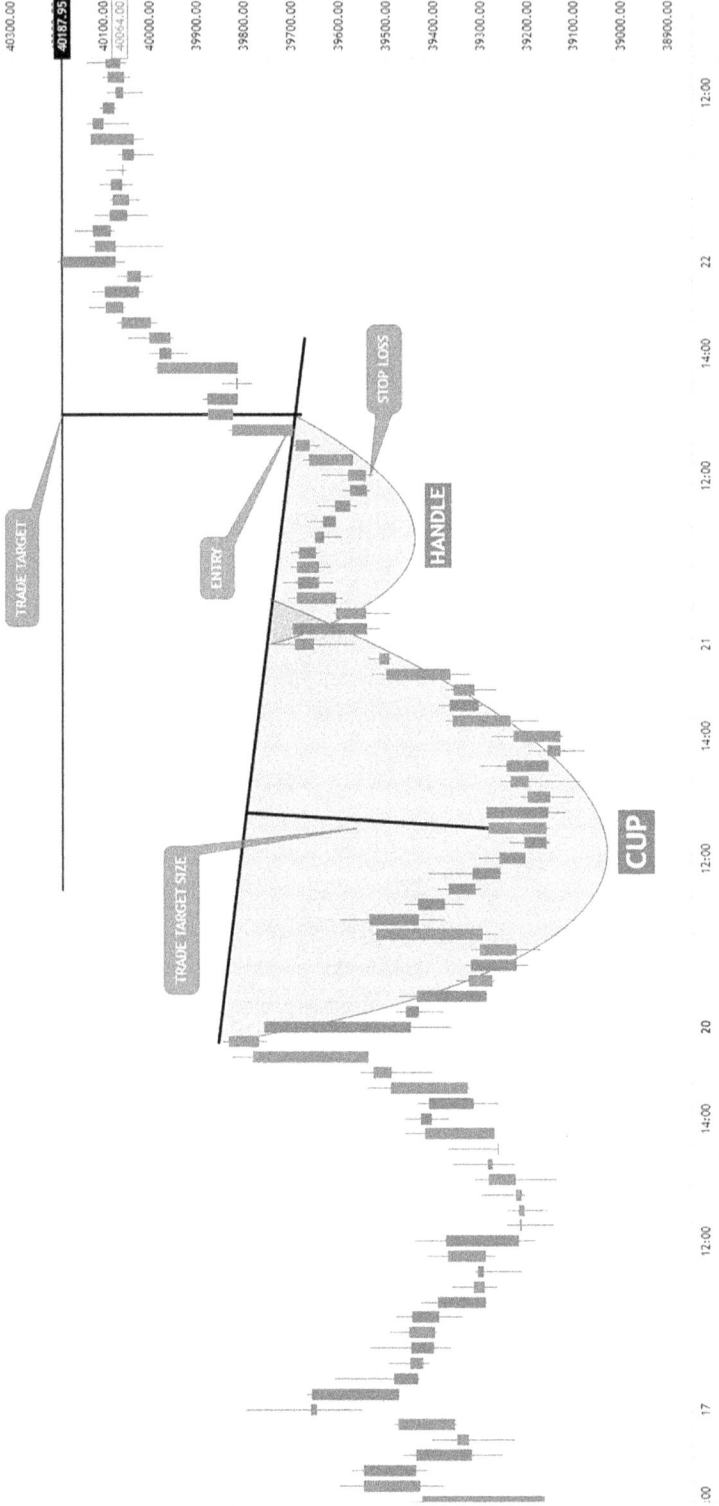

M- Pattern

Imagine you're at a party and you're having a great time - the music is pumping, the drinks are flowing, and everyone is dancing. But then, suddenly, the party takes a turn for the worse. The music slows down, the lights dim, and people start to leave. This is a lot like the M pattern in financial markets!

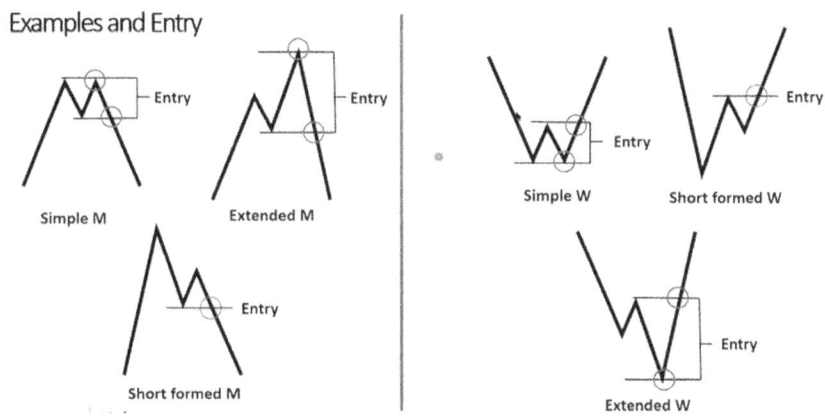

Examples and Entry

The M pattern is a bearish technical analysis tool that traders use to identify potential trend reversals. The pattern gets its name from its distinctive shape, which looks like the letter "M." The pattern is formed when an asset's price rises to a high point and then falls back down, creating a trough. The price then rises again, but not as high as the previous high, forming the middle peak of the M shape. Finally, the price falls once again, breaking through the previous trough and signalling a potential downtrend.

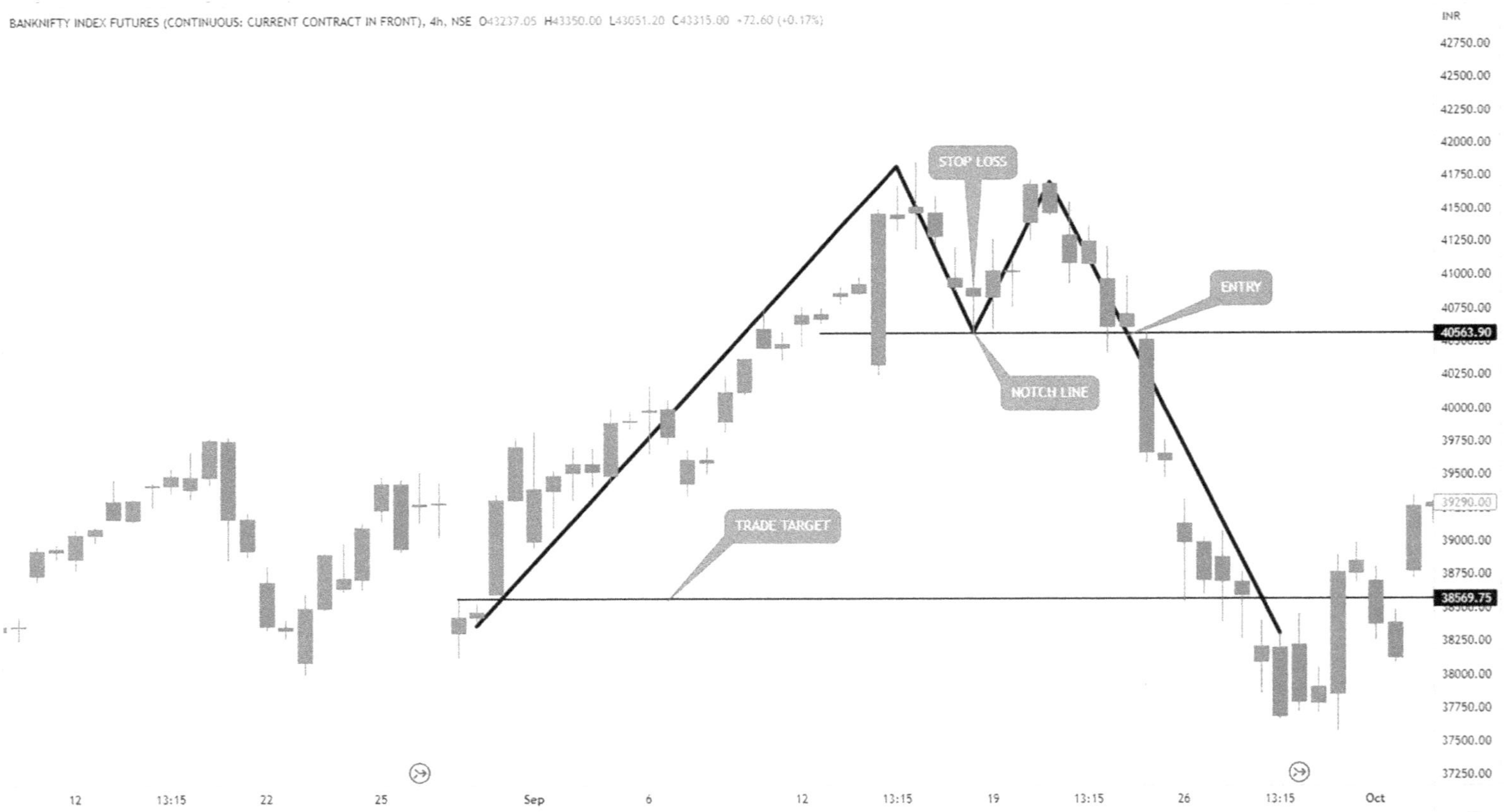
BANKNIFTY INDEX FUTURES (CONTINUOUS: CURRENT CONTRACT IN FRONT), 4h, NSE O43237.05 H43350.00 L43051.20 C43315.00 +72.60 (+0.17%)
INR
42750.00
42500.00
42250.00
42000.00
41750.00
41500.00
41250.00
41000.00
40750.00
40563.90
40250.00
40000.00
39750.00
39500.00
39290.00
39000.00
38750.00
38569.75
38250.00
38000.00
37750.00
37500.00
37250.00
STOP LOSS
NOTCH LINE
ENTRY
TRADE TARGET
12
13:15
22
25
Sep
6
12
13:15
19
13:15
26
13:15
Oct

When traders spot the M pattern, they may look to enter a short position, selling the asset in the hopes that the price will continue to fall. However, it's important to note that not every M pattern will lead to a profitable trade, and traders should always use other indicators and analysis tools to confirm the validity of the pattern.

W – pattern

W pattern is a powerful tool that traders use to identify potential trend reversals in the financial markets. It's called the W pattern because of its distinctive shape, which resembles the letter "W". This pattern can be a reliable signal for traders looking to enter a long position and profit from an upcoming bullish trend.

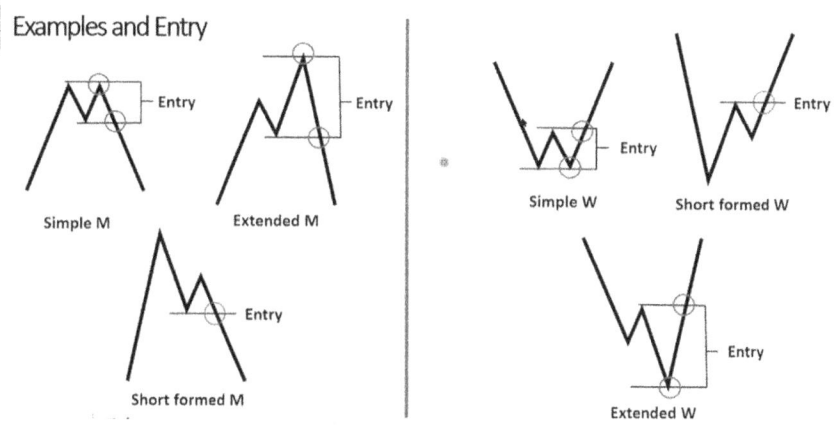

When traders spot the W pattern, they look for a specific set of conditions that confirm its validity. These conditions include two distinct lows separated by a higher low in the middle, forming the characteristic "W" shape. Traders will also look for other technical indicators, such as moving averages and volume levels, to confirm the pattern and make informed trading decisions.

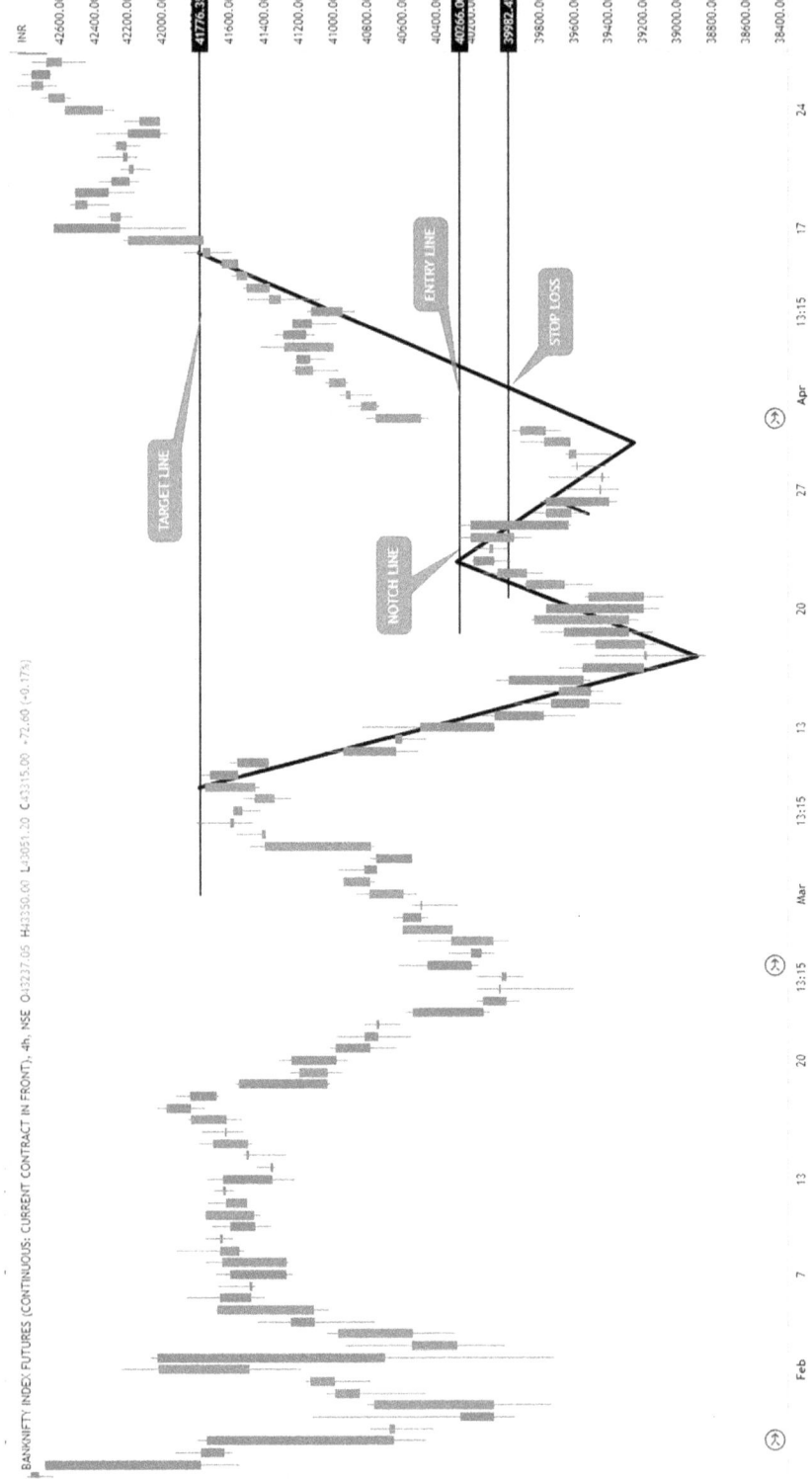

CHAPTER

12   5 STAR SETUP

Trading Strategies

Trading without a strategy is like wandering through a dense jungle blindfolded – you might stumble upon a hidden gem or get bitten by a venomous snake. It's a gamble, and not one you should take with your hard-earned cash.

To avoid getting lost in the jungle, you need a map and a compass. Your trading strategy is your map – it shows you where to go and how to get there. Your indicators and tools are your compass – they guide you through the twists and turns of the market.

But don't just follow someone else's map – make your own! A trading strategy that is tailored to your unique needs and risk tolerance is more likely to lead you to treasure than a one-size-fits-all approach.

And don't forget to pack a survival kit – aka risk management. Set stop-loss orders, use trailing stops, and don't risk more than you can afford to lose. It's better to come back with a few scraps than to end up stranded in the jungle.

Remember, even the best strategy won't work if you don't have the discipline to follow it. Stick to your plan, resist the urge to chase shiny objects, and avoid making impulsive trades based on FOMO (Fear Of Missing Out).

In the end, developing a trading strategy takes time and effort, but it's worth it. It gives you a sense of direction, a safety net, and the confidence to take calculated risks. So grab your compass, put on your adventurer's hat, and get ready to discover the hidden treasures of the market!

1. KAILASHA HACK

Welcome to the world of Kailasha Hack - TWT's Morning Breakfast Strategy! It's a powerful technique that works wonders on Bank Nifty and helps us start our day on a profitable note. Let's take a journey together and explore the rules of this magical strategy.

The Kailasha Hack is designed specifically for Bank Nifty.

To implement this strategy, we need to use the 5-minute time frame.

As a trader, you can choose to buy or sell futures or ITM call/put options based on the entry signals.

It's important to manage risk and reward at all times. We recommend that you never invest more than 25% of your trading capital in a single trade.

You can submit multiple entries until 11:00 AM. After that, we will not accept any trades using the Kailasha Hack after 11 AM.

Preparation is key to the success of this strategy. Here's what you need to do:

On a 5-minute chart, mark the high and low of the last 5-minute candle from the previous day (3:25 PM to 3:30 PM).

If the market opens with a gap up from the previous day, we will take the trade on the sell side (PUT) and wait for the sell entry in the form of a breakdown of the levels marked in the morning.

If the market opens with a gap down, we will take the trade on the buy side (CALL) and wait for the buy side entry in the form of a breakout of the levels marked in the morning.

Now, let's talk about targets. We recommend that you aim for the following targets:

1st target: 45 points from the entry

2nd target: 70 points from the entry

3rd target: 90 points from the entry

4th target: 120 points from the entry

Finally, let's discuss stop loss. You must always be prepared to cut your losses to minimize risk. Here are the stop loss rules:

In case of a buy trade, the low of yesterday's last 5-minute candle will be the stop loss.

In case of a sell trade, the high of yesterday's last 5-minute candle will be the stop loss.

With the Kailasha Hack in your trading arsenal, you're well on your way to achieving greater profits and success in the exciting world of trading. Happy trading!

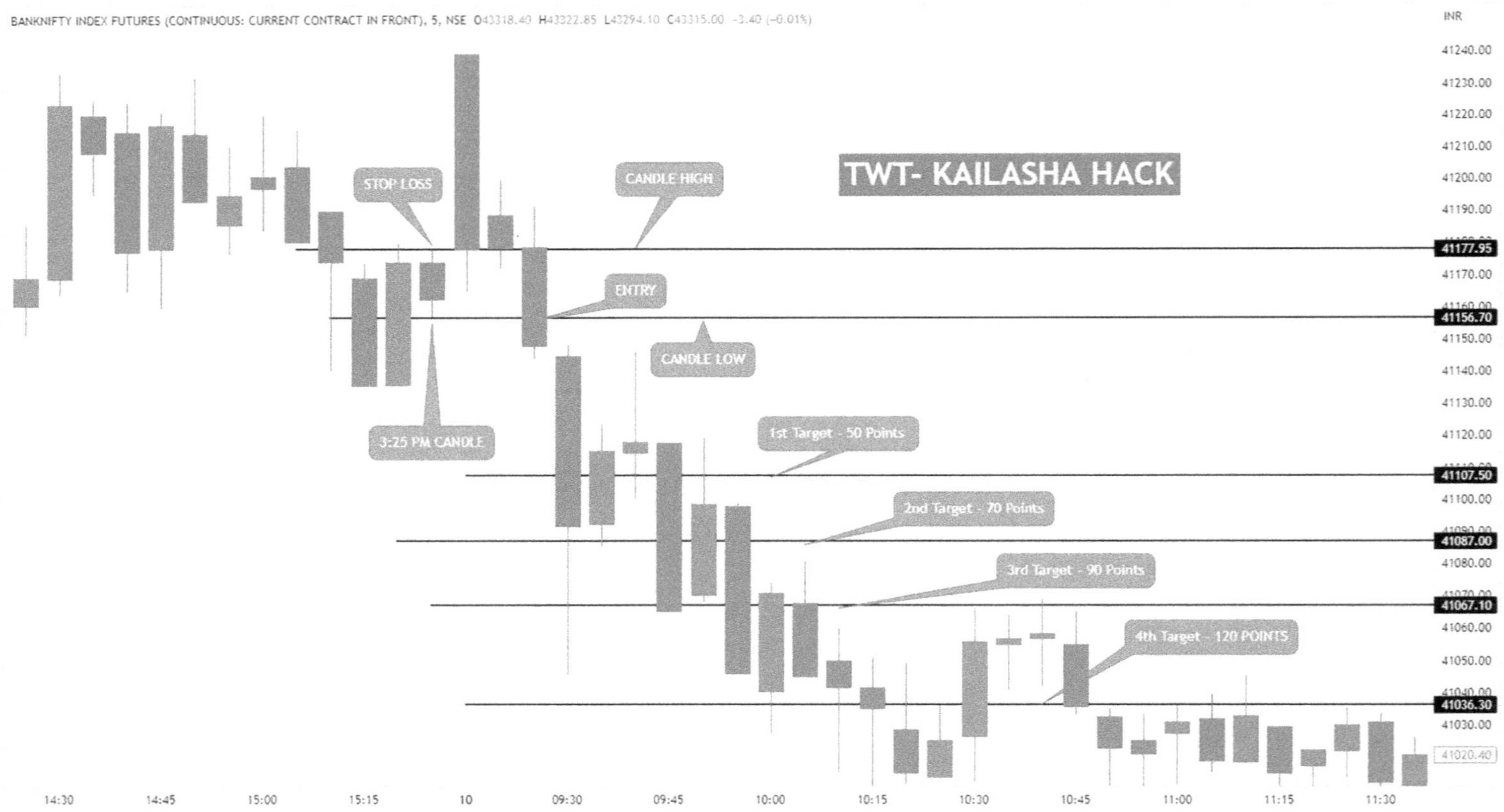
BANKNIFTY INDEX FUTURES (CONTINUOUS: CURRENT CONTRACT IN FRONT), 5, NSE O43318.40 H43322.85 L43294.10 C43315.00 -3.40 (-0.01%)
TWT- KAILASHA HACK
STOP LOSS
CANDLE HIGH
ENTRY
CANDLE LOW
3:25 PM CANDLE
1st Target - 50 Points
2nd Target - 70 Points
3rd Target - 90 Points
4th Target - 120 POINTS
INR
41240.00
41230.00
41220.00
41210.00
41200.00
41190.00
41177.95
41170.00
41156.70
41150.00
41140.00
41130.00
41120.00
41107.50
41100.00
41087.00
41080.00
41067.10
41060.00
41050.00
41036.30
41030.00
41020.40
14:30
14:45
15:00
15:15
10
09:30
09:45
10:00
10:15
10:30
10:45
11:00
11:15
11:30

2. DAY TRADING 5-MINUTE BREAKOUT STRATEGY

1. If you're looking for a tried-and-true trading strategy that doesn't rely on indicators, the 5-minute breakout strategy might be just what you need. It's been around for a while, but it's still highly effective in identifying opening ranges and profiting from breakouts.
2. What's great about this strategy is that it's straightforward and easy to understand. You don't need to be a seasoned trader to master it – even beginners can quickly pick it up and start making consistent profits.
3. And the best part? You don't need any fancy tools or indicators to make it work. All you need is a chart and some basic knowledge of price action.
4. So, if you're ready to take your trading to the next level, it's time to learn the 5-minute breakout strategy. With dedication and practice, you can become a pro at spotting breakout opportunities and making smart trades that lead to steady profits.

Process for the 5 min breakout strategy:

1. Wait for the first 5-minute candle to form in the Bank Nifty 5-minute time frame.
2. Mark the high and low points of the candle and establish the range.
3. Wait for the breakout or breakdown of the candle.
4. Keep your target at 50 to 80 points or a 1:2 Risk & Reward Trade.
5. The stop-loss (SL) can be set at the low of the candle in case of a breakout and at the high of the candle in case of a breakdown on a closing basis.
6. The entry of the trade will happen on a closing candle basis as well.
7. Note that the above strategy is only for Bank Nifty.
8. Avoid the trade if the first 5-minute candle is above 150 points.

Trade Example

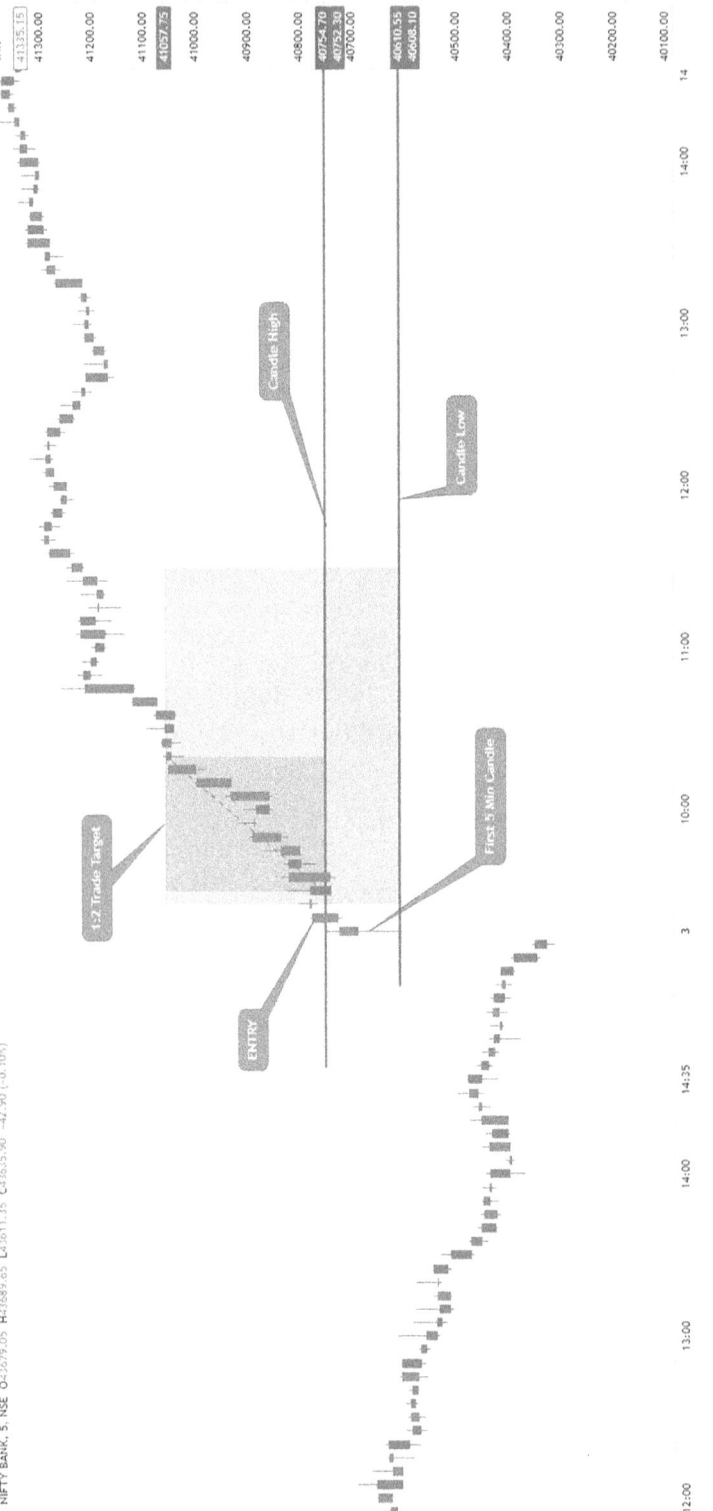

More than 200 point candle - NO TRADE.

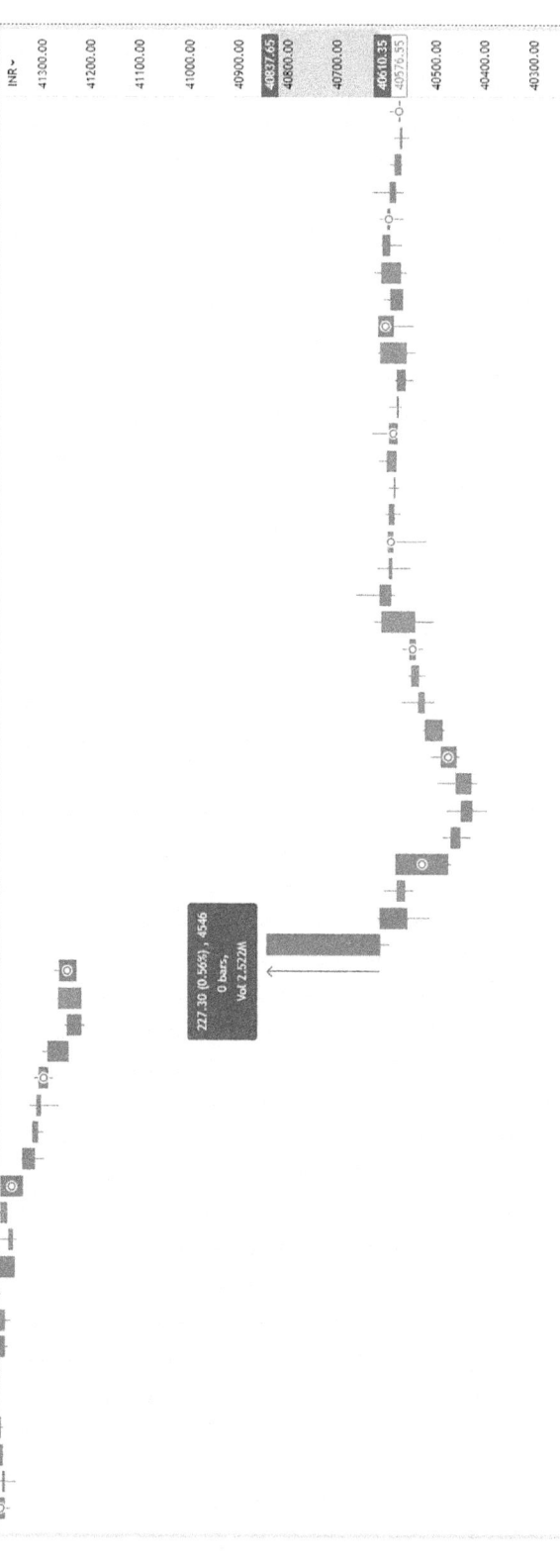

3. TWT – 333 STRATEGY FOR BANK NIFTY

Welcome to the world of trading, where making a profit is like finding a needle in a haystack. But not anymore! I'm going to let you in on a little secret that will change your trading game forever - the 333 hack!

This hack is so simple yet so effective that you'll wonder why you didn't know about it before. It's based on pure price action and works wonders on Bank Nifty instruments. All you need to do is follow the rules, and you'll see your monthly PNL turn green in no time!

Are you ready to learn a powerful day trading strategy that can help you boost your profits and take your trading to the next level? Look no further than the 333 hack, a pure price action-based strategy that works wonders in the Bank Nifty market.

Follow these simple rules to ensure that you execute the strategy correctly:

1. This strategy is designed to work with Bank Nifty instruments only.
2. Always use a 3-minute timeframe on the chart.
3. Check the India VIX. If it is below 17, do not use this strategy for the day.
4. When the market opens, wait for the third candle on the 3-minute chart.
5. Mark the high and low of the candle as soon as it closes.
6. Measure the size of the candle quickly.
7. If the candle size is less than 65, take the trade. Otherwise, do not use this strategy for the day.

Here's how to execute the trade:

1. Mark the high and low of the third candle on the 3-minute timeframe in Bank Nifty.
2. If any candle closes above the marked candle high, take the buy trade.
3. If any candle closes below the low of the marked candle, take the sell trade.
4. Always buy in-the-money (ITM) or at-the-money (ATM) option calls. However, for the best results, it is always recommended to buy the Future.
5. Set your target for the trade at a 1:3 risk and reward ratio for both sides. For example, if the candle size is 40 points, the target points should be 120.
6. "Place your stop loss for the strategy at the high of the marked candle for sell trades and at the low of the candle for buy trades."

I've been using this strategy for the past five years, and it has helped me achieve financial freedom and accumulate substantial wealth. Let's see how the 333 hack can help you achieve your trading goals too!

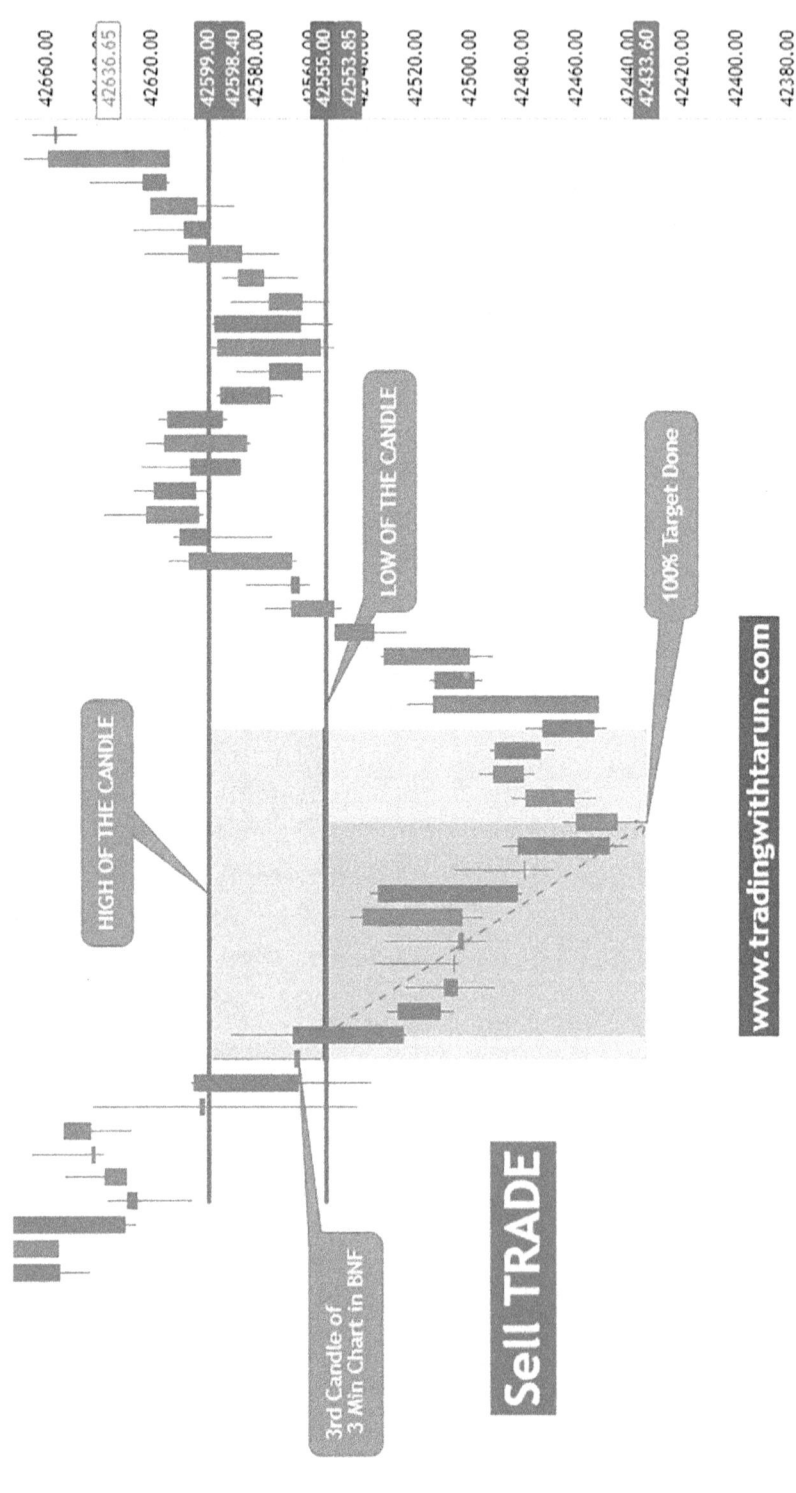

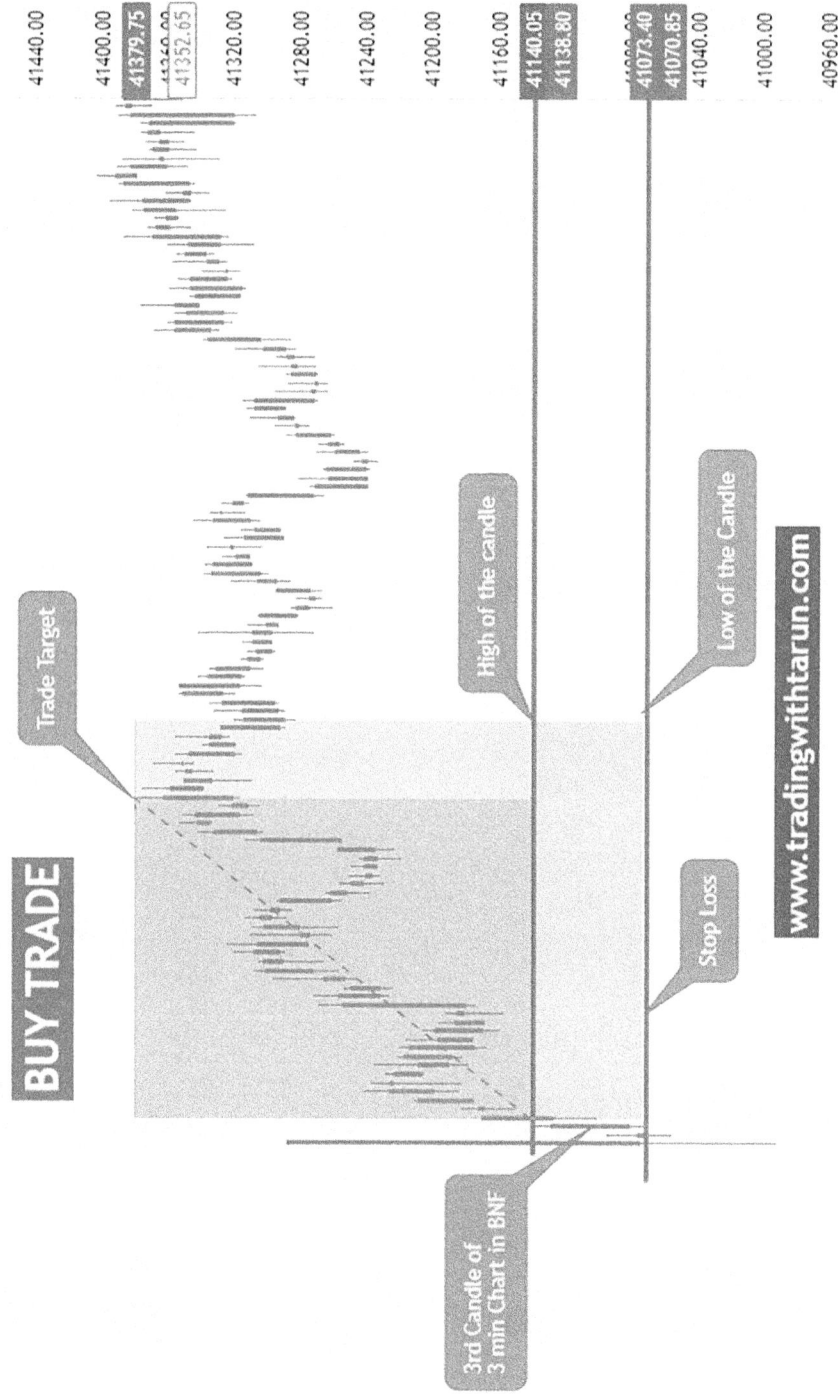

4. 245 HACK FOR DAY TRADER'S

As you all know, trading in the stock market can be a roller coaster ride. But what if I told you that there's a strategy that guarantees you profits during the closing hours? Yes, you heard it right! It's called the 245 hack, and it's TWT's secret weapon to end the trading day on a high note. With this strategy, your monthly P&L will always be in the green.

Here are the steps to using this amazing strategy:

This strategy is only for Bank Nifty, so please keep that in mind.

We will use a 15-minute time frame for this strategy.

You can buy or sell futures or ITM call/put options, depending on your preference.

Remember to manage your risk and reward and never use more than 25% of your trading capital in one trade.

Now, let's move on to the preparation steps:

Wait for the candle to form from 2:45 pm to 3:00 pm.

Mark the high and low of the 15-minute candle from 2:45 pm to 3:00 pm.

Trade the breakout or breakdown of the candle after 3:00 pm.

To ensure your profits, set your targets as follows:

1st target: 45 points from the entry

2nd target: 70 points from the entry

3rd target: 90 points from the entry

4th target: 120 points from the entry

And last but not least, the stop loss:

In case of a buy trade, the low of the 15-minute candle will be the stop loss.

In case of a sell trade, the high of the 15-minute candle will be the stop loss.

So, there you have it, folks! With the 245 hack, you can end your trading day with profits and a big smile on your face. Happy trading!

BANKNIFTY INDEX FUTURES (CONTINUOUS; CURRENT CONTRACT IN FRONT), 15, NSE O:43331.70 H:43342.00 L:43294.10 C:43315.00 -16.05 (-0.04%)

Chart annotations:
- TARGET
- ENTRY: 43240.60
- STOP LOSS: 43170.50
- CANDLE HIGH
- CANDLE LOW
- 43315.00

330 FORMULA – "SANJEEVANI STRATEGY"

As a day trader, you're probably always looking for ways to make quick money, right? Well, there's a strategy out there that could be the answer to your prayers. It's called the "330 Sanjeevni Formula," and it can help you predict Index Gap up and Gap Down like a pro every single day.

Now, before you get too excited, let's remember that with every strategy comes its own set of risks and rewards. The key is to approach this with proper logic and not treat it like a gamble. If you do this, you can make regular profits and see some serious green in your account.

So, what is the 330 Sanjeevni formula?

Process:

1. Use two EMAs on the chart - the 5 EMA and 15 EMA
2. Ensure that the 5 EMA is green and the 15 EMA is red in color.
3. Use a 5-minute time frame to apply this formula
4. Watch the index at 3:25 pm to find the gap up or gap down.
5. If the Green Line (5EMA) is above the Red Line (15EMA), it means there will be a gap up tomorrow.
6. If the Red line (15 EMA) is above the Green line (5 EMA), it means there will be a Gap Down tomorrow.
7. Buy "in the money" strike price or index future at 3:29 pm for maximum profit.
8. Never buy an out-of-the-money (OTM) strike price.
9. Exit the trade in the morning in small or big green.

GAP UP Example – Bank nifty

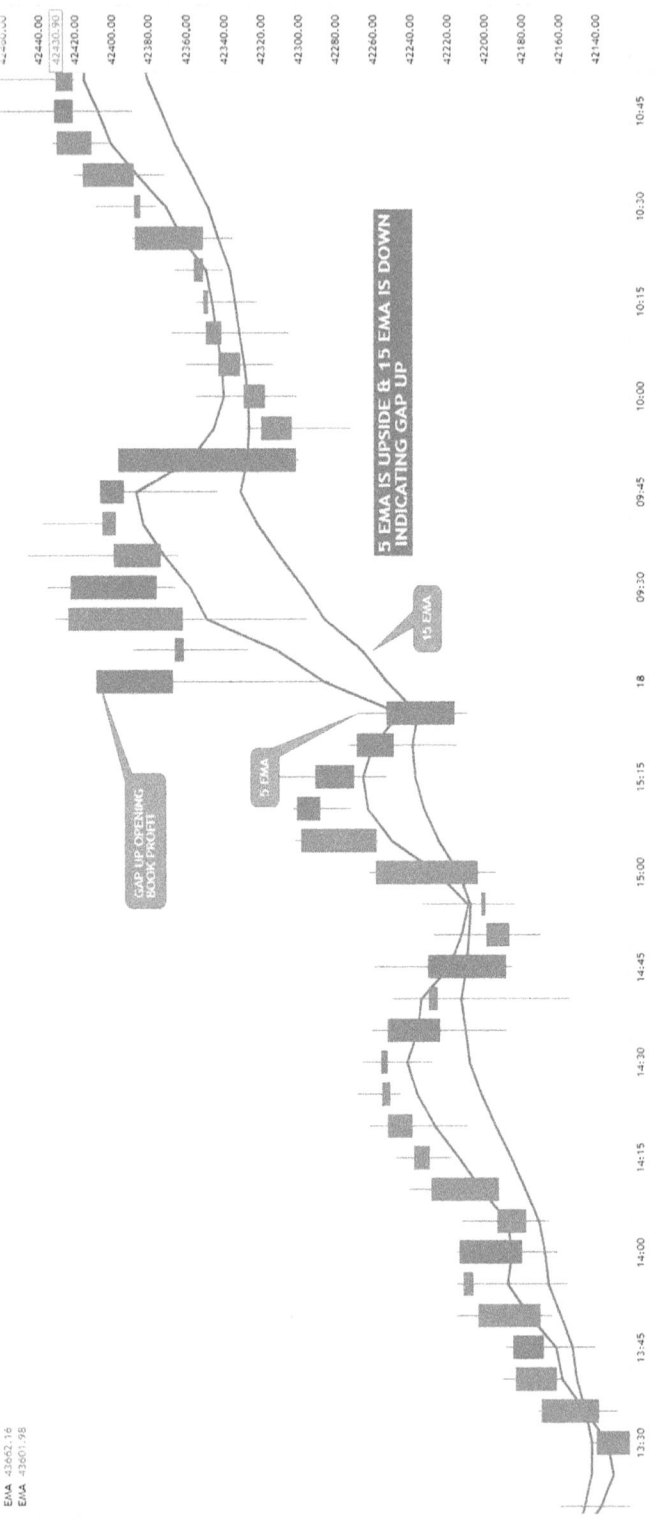

GAP Down Example – Bank nifty

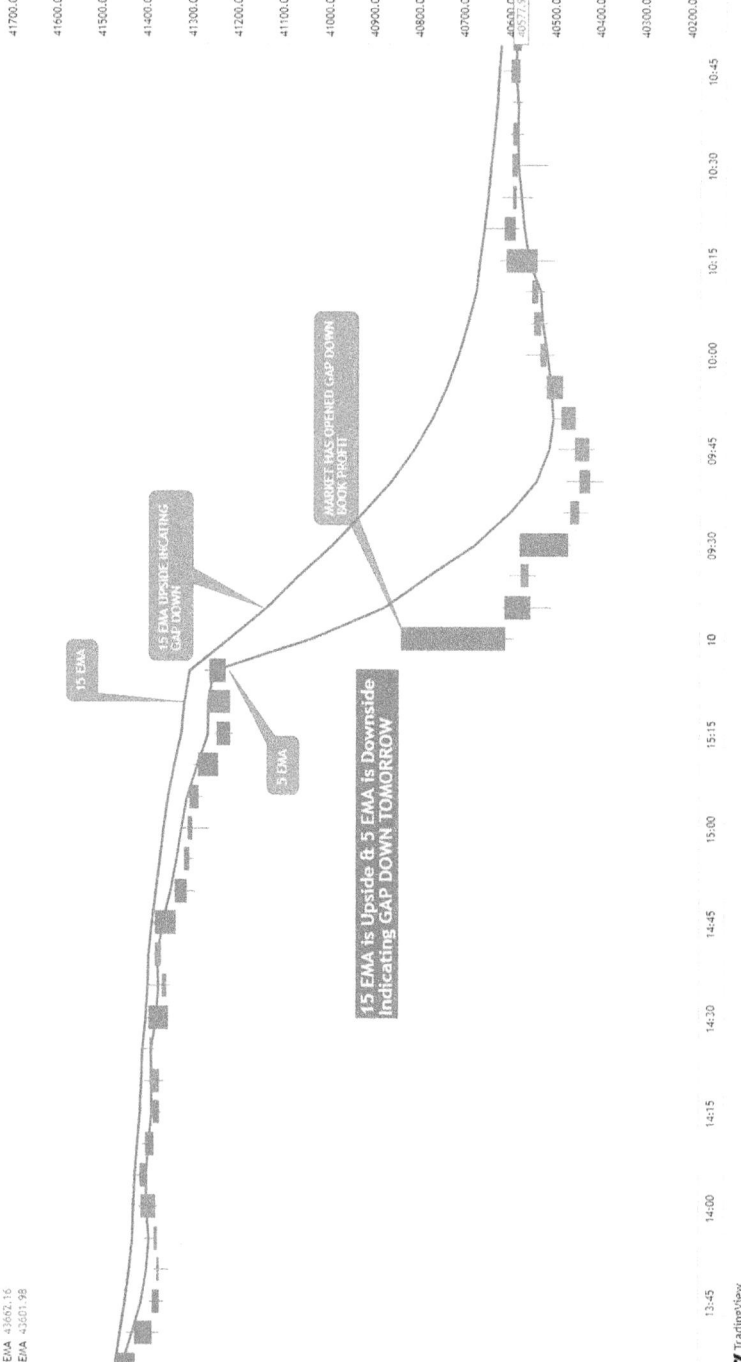

Pro tips:

1. Check all 3 indices - Nifty, Bank Nifty, and CNX Nifty.
2. If all three indicate one side move, it's better
3. If they indicate different side moves, choose the move reflected in at least 2 out of 3 indexes. For example, if NIFTY and BNF are indicating a gap down, but CNX Nifty is indicating a gap up, then choose the gap down option.

Risk and position management:

It is essential to manage your position sizing in advance to avoid regrets later. Invest no more than 30% of your trading capital in one trade ever. Always manage your position sizing in a way that you have money to average your trade, so you are not caught off guard.

Trade management:

As a trader, you know that the market can be unpredictable, and even the best analysis can sometimes go wrong. That's why it's crucial to have a trade management plan in place. In case the market opens against your position, you need a Plan B. One effective strategy is to average your trade with the same amount of quantity you're already holding.

For example, if you're holding 2 lots and the market opens against your analysis, buy 2 more lots of the same quantity to average out your trade. If you're holding 5 lots, buy 5 more lots to average it out.

But here's the key: we don't just sit and wait for the market to turn in our favor indefinitely. We set a maximum time limit of 11 am and exit the trade as soon as we're in the green profit. This way, we're able to manage risk effectively and optimize our profits. With a solid trade management plan like this, you'll be well on your way to success in the trading world.

Trade management when the market opens against our analysis

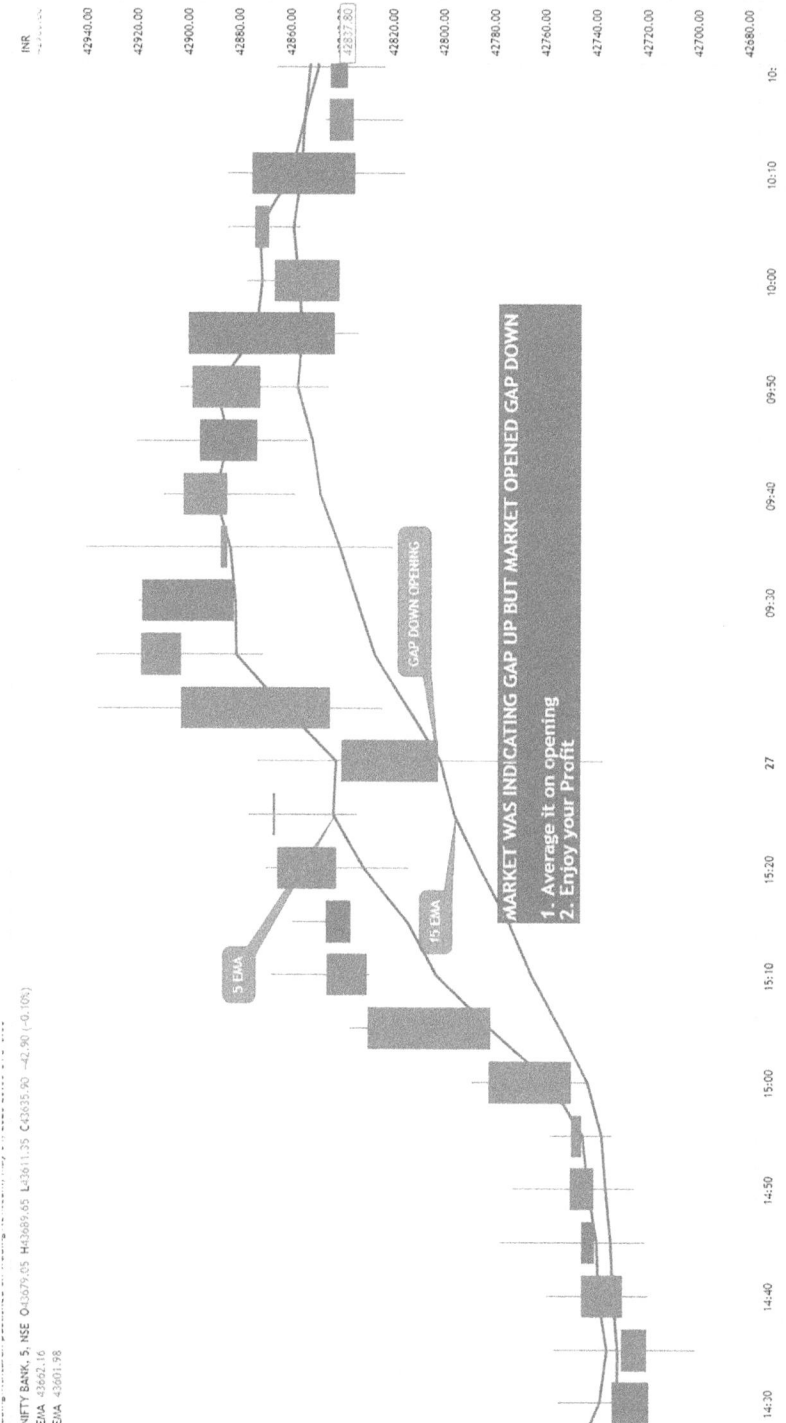

Strategy Accuracy %:

The accuracy of this strategy is between 70%-80%, meaning that every 10 trades you take, 7-8 will end up in profit, and your overall monthly positions will be in good green numbers.

By following the 330 Sanjeevni Formula and incorporating the pro tips and risk management strategies, you can increase your chances of consistent profits and make the most of your day trading opportunities.

BONUS CONTENT FOR OUR BOOK READERS AND STUDENTS BY TWT

CHAPTER 13

MSM CONCEPT

Once upon a time, in a small village nestled in a valley, there was a farmer named Jack. Jack worked hard every day to tend to his crops, but he often faced challenges from pests, weather, and other factors that threatened to damage his harvest.

One day, Jack noticed that a large tree had fallen across the path leading to his farm. He knew he needed to clear the tree to ensure his crops could be brought to market on time. But as he tried to move the tree, he realized it was too heavy for him to lift alone.

Just as he was about to give up, he heard a voice calling out to him from the other side of the tree. It was a wise old man, who offered to help Jack move the tree in exchange for a share of his harvest.

Together, they were able to move the tree and clear the path. Jack was grateful for the old man's help, and he asked him how he knew so much about strength and leverage. The old man replied that he had learned about it through studying support and resistance in the stock market.

He went on to explain that just as the tree provided support for Jack's crops and resistance to their movement, support and resistance levels in the stock market could provide guidance for traders in predicting the direction of the market.

Jack was intrigued, and the old man offered to teach him more about support and resistance in the stock market. Over time, Jack became an expert in using support and resistance levels to make profitable trades, and he was able to expand his farm and grow his business.

The lesson Jack learned was that just as he needed support to move the fallen tree, traders needed support and resistance levels to guide their decisions in the stock market. And with the right knowledge and tools, anyone could become a successful trader.

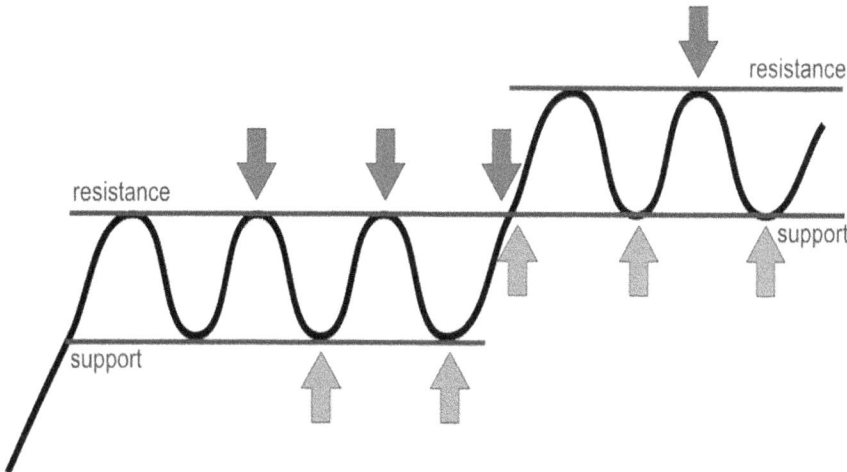

TYPE OF SUPPORT & RESISTANCE

One of the most essential concepts in technical analysis is horizontal support and resistance. Traders use this concept to identify crucial price levels in the financial markets that signal buying or selling pressure for an asset.

Imagine you're hiking up a steep mountain, with a rocky trail beneath your feet. As you make your way up the trail, you notice that there are certain spots where the rocks seem to be more worn down than others. These spots feel almost flat and level, as if other hikers have stopped there to take a break.

Now, imagine that the mountain is actually the financial markets, and the rocky trail represents the price movements of an asset. These "flat" spots on the trail are like the horizontal support and resistance levels that traders look for on a price chart.

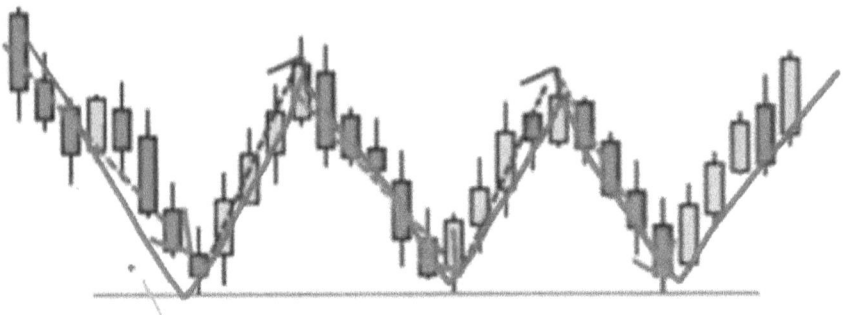

When an asset's price approaches a support level, it's like hikers taking a break on a level part of the trail. Buyers see the asset as undervalued and jump in, creating buying pressure that can push the price back up. On the other hand, when an asset's price approaches a resistance level, it's like hikers reaching a steep and rocky incline. Sellers see the asset as overvalued and start to sell, creating selling pressure that can push the price back down.

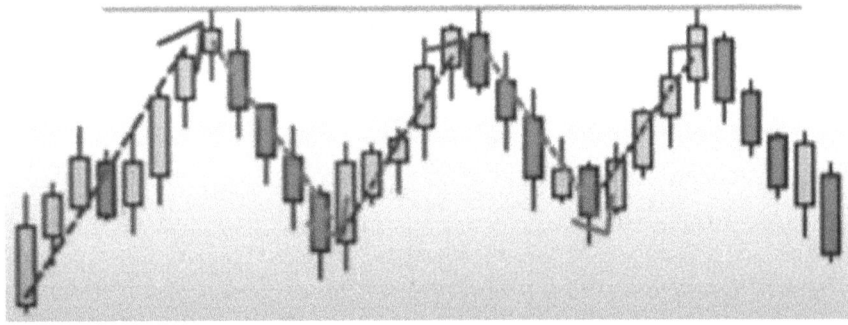

Of course, just like hiking, trading is not always smooth sailing. Sometimes the trail is too rocky to find a good resting spot, or the weather turns bad and hikers have to turn back. Similarly, support and resistance levels are not always reliable, and traders should use additional analysis tools to confirm their validity.

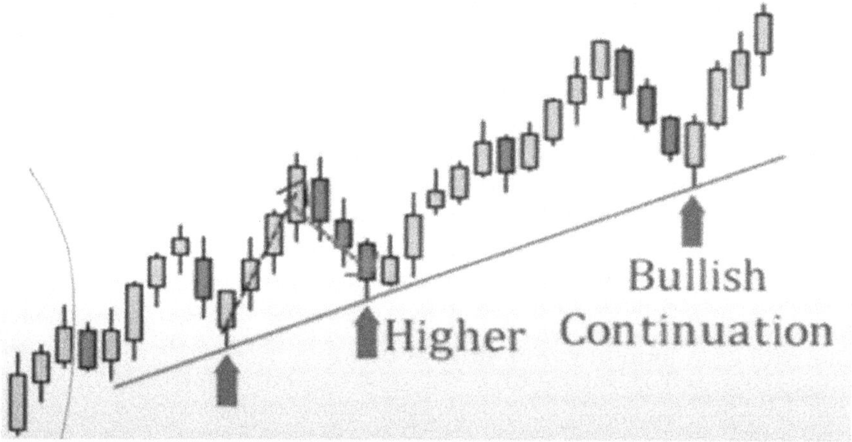

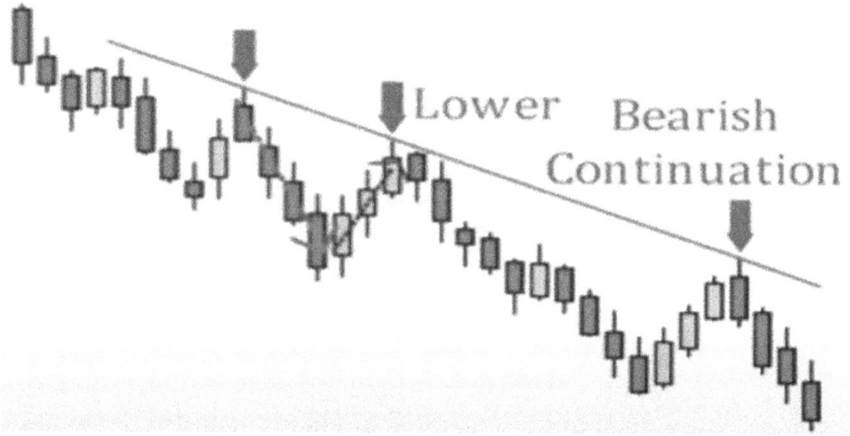

Buying with Horizontal Support

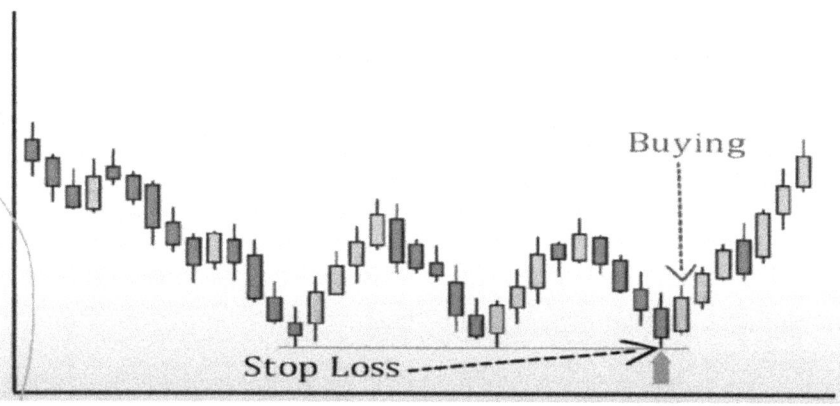

You've already mastered the art of identifying support and resistance levels, and now it's time to put that knowledge into action!

Picture this: A trading approach that revolves around the mystical allure of trendlines. With the MSM strategy, we're about to take your trading experience to a whole new level.

Let's break it down. The MSM strategy is all about the magic of three touches on a trendline. Pay close attention because this is where the real excitement begins.

The first touch is marked by the letter "M" representing the "MINOR" level. It's like the gentle tap on the shoulder that catches your attention.

The second touch is where things start to get serious. We use the letter "S" to symbolize the "STRONG" level. It's as if the trendline is flexing its muscles, demanding your full focus.

But wait, there's more! The third touch is the grand finale, and it's labelled with another "M," but this time it stands for "MAJOR." This touch signifies a significant turning point in the trendline's journey.

Now that you understand the three-touch rule, it's time to unleash your trading prowess. Find two points where the trendline is touched and patiently wait for that exhilarating third touch. When it comes to selling, embrace the power of rejection. And when it comes to buying, seek solace in the arms of support.

Once you've identified your rejection or support candle, it's time to strike. Enter the trade with confidence, setting your sights on a remarkable 1:3 risk-reward ratio. That's right, let your dreams soar as you aim for three times the profit you risked!

Trade Example

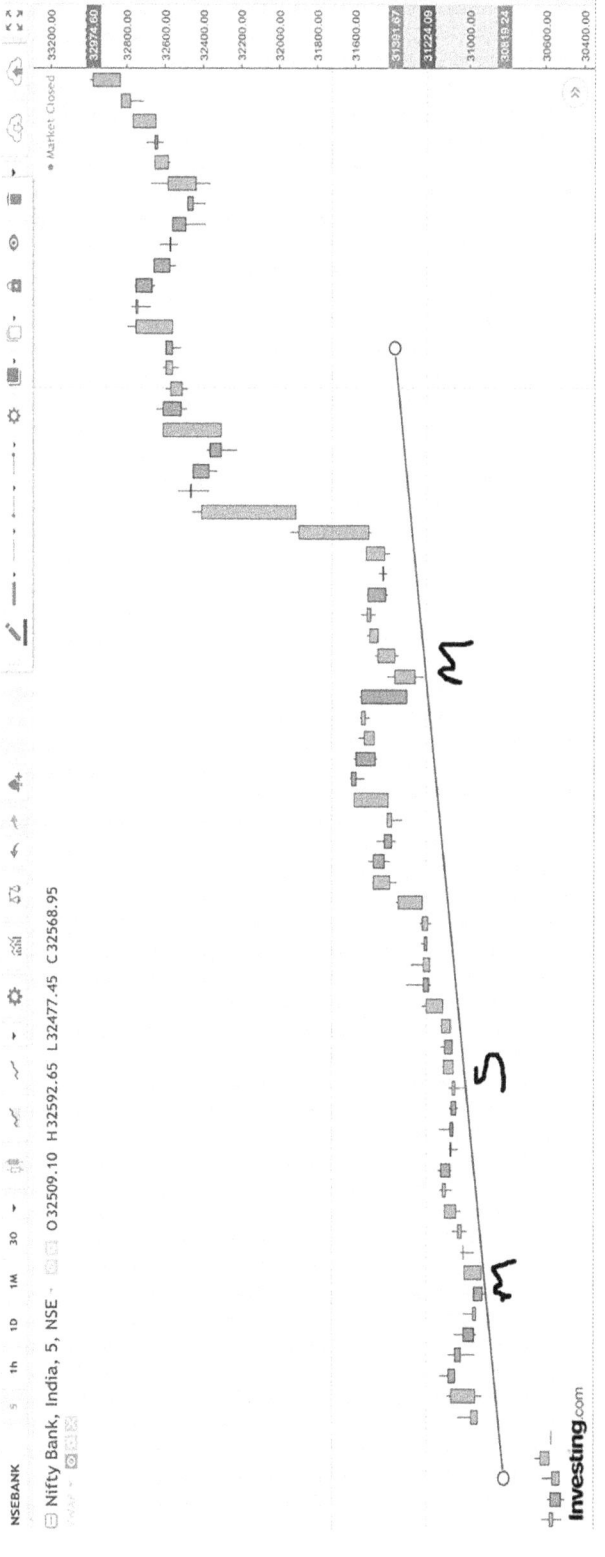

But don't forget, every superhero needs a safety net. In a sell trade, the high of the rejection candle becomes your stop loss. And in a buy trade, the low of the support candle acts as your shield. With these safeguards in place, you can trade fearlessly, knowing that you're protected.

Of course, no strategy is complete without sound money management. As you embark on your trading journey, always remember to follow prudent money management principles. They will serve as your guiding compass, keeping you on track toward success.

Now, here's the truly remarkable part. The MSM strategy is a versatile powerhouse that can be applied across any timeframe, any market, and any instrument. That's right, the possibilities are endless. Whether you're trading stocks, forex, or cryptocurrencies, the MSM strategy is your trusted companion.

So, are you ready to unlock the full potential of trendlines? Embrace the MSM strategy and get ready to witness the awe-inspiring transformation of your trading endeavors. Get out there and conquer the markets like never before!

Disclaimer: Trading involves risk, and it's important to do thorough research and seek professional advice before engaging in any trading activities.

Trade Example

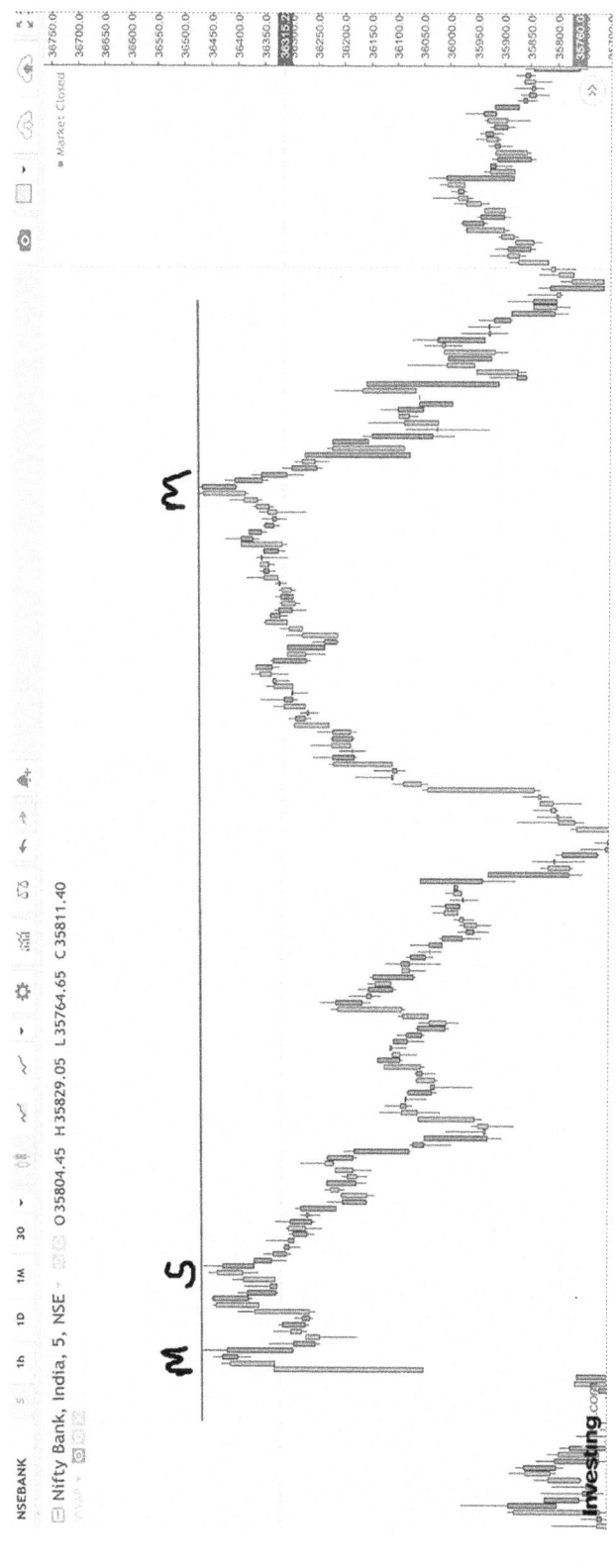

Trade Example

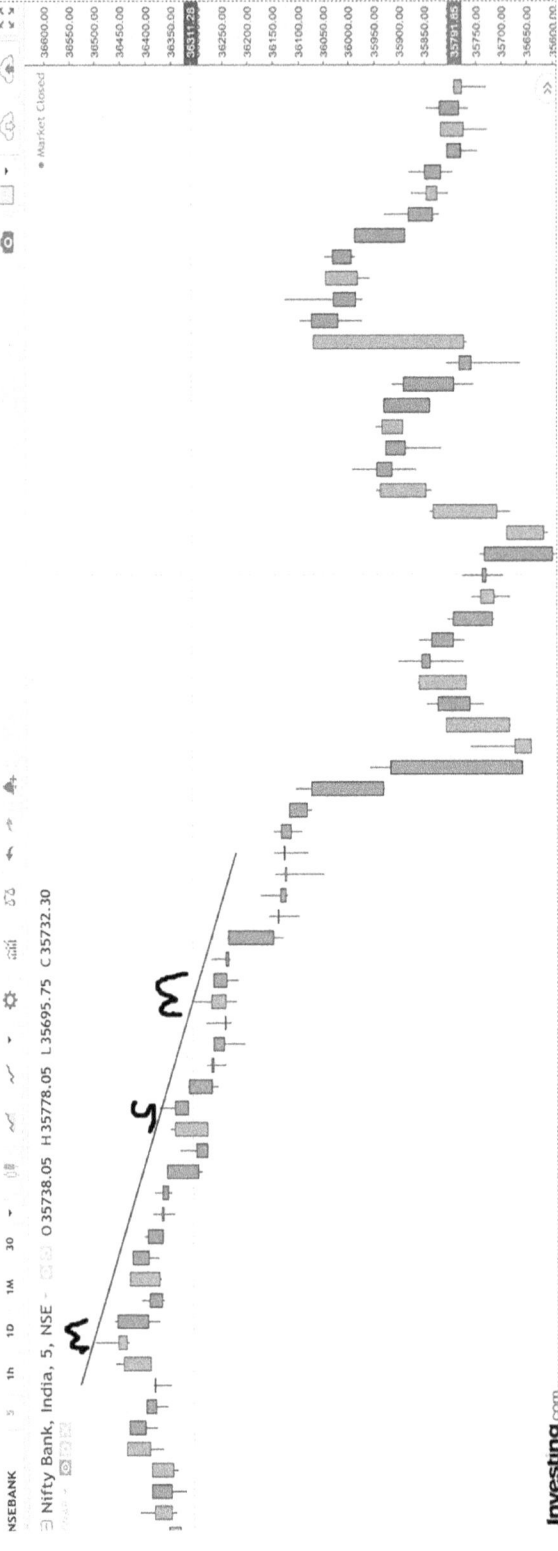

CHAPTER 14
TRADER DAILY RITUALS

A successful trader's routine is crucial for achieving consistent profits in the world of trading. Here are some key elements that can make up a successful trader's routine:

1. Start with a morning routine: A successful trader always starts their day with a healthy breakfast, exercise, and meditation or mindfulness practice. This helps them stay focused and calm throughout the day.
2. Review the market news: Before the market opens, a trader should review the latest market news and economic reports. This helps them stay informed about any potential market-moving events.
3. Check the charts: A trader should analyze the charts of their preferred trading instruments, looking for any potential trading opportunities. This may involve using technical analysis tools and indicators.
4. Plan the trades: Based on the market analysis, a trader should plan his or her trades for the day, including entry and exit points, stop loss levels, and position sizing. This helps him or her to execute trades with confidence and discipline.
5. Execute the trades: During the trading session, a trader should focus on executing his or her trades according to his or her plan, while also keeping an eye on the market for any unexpected developments.
6. Review and reflect: At the end of the trading session, a trader should review their trades and reflect on their performance. This

can help them to identify any mistakes or areas for improvement, as well as to celebrate their successes.

7. Keep learning: A successful trader is always learning and expanding their knowledge of the

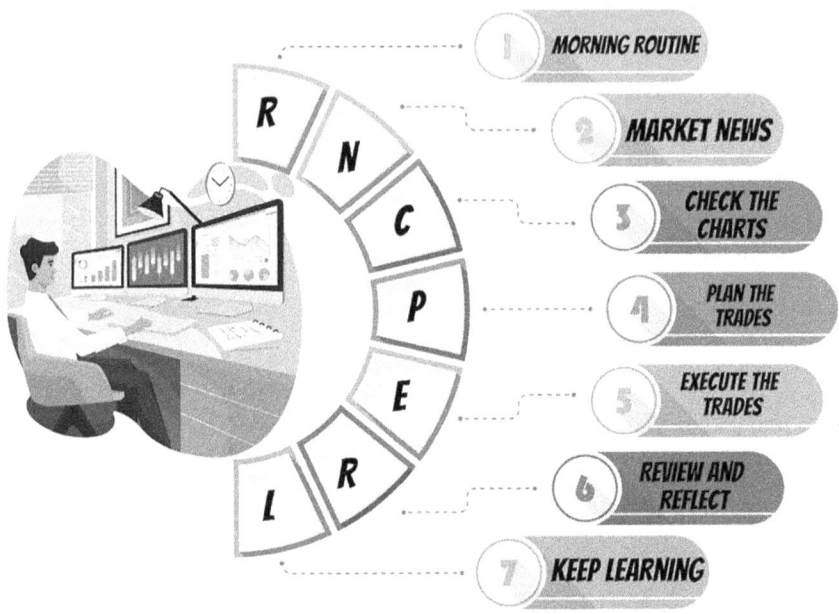

CHAPTER 15
THE POWER OF TRADING PSYCHOLOGY

The Importance of Understanding Your Emotions in Trading

Emotions play a crucial role in trading. They can drive decisions, both good and bad, and can have a significant impact on your trading performance. Understanding your emotions is the first step in mastering them. In this chapter, we will explore the different emotions that traders experience, such as fear, greed, and anxiety, and how they can affect trading decisions. We will also discuss the importance of emotional awareness and how to develop it through self-reflection and journaling.

As a trader, it's important to recognize that your emotions are not your enemy. Emotions are a natural and necessary part of being human, and they can be a valuable source of information in trading. By learning to recognize and manage your emotions, you can use them to your advantage and make better trading decisions. We will also discuss the impact of cognitive biases on trading psychology and how to identify and overcome them.

Ultimately, the goal of this chapter is to help you understand the importance of emotional intelligence in trading and to provide you with the tools to develop it. With emotional intelligence, you can better manage your emotions and make informed trading decisions that align with your trading goals.

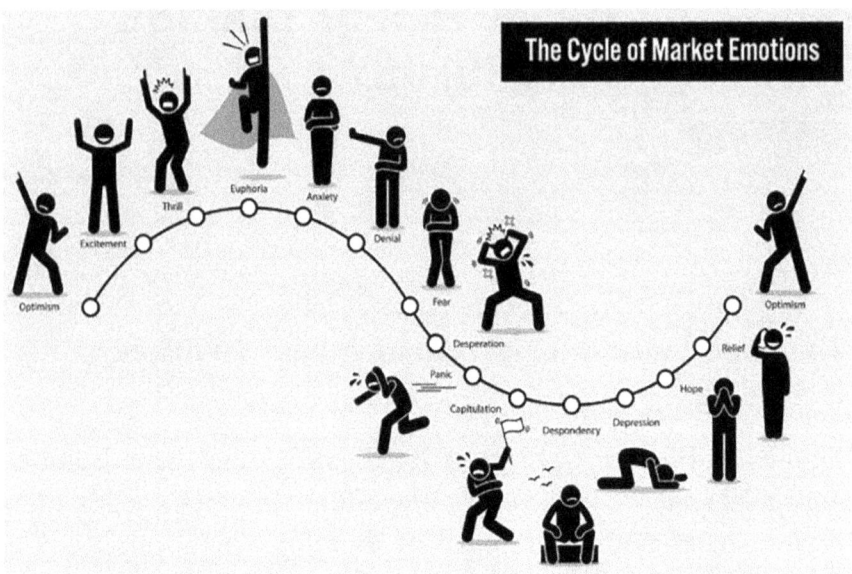

The Psychological Aspects of Risk Management

Risk management is a crucial aspect of trading, but it's not only about managing financial risks. Psychological risks also play a significant role in trading and can have a negative impact on your trading performance. In this chapter, we will delve into the psychological aspects of risk management and learn how to recognize and handle psychological hazards.

The first step in managing psychological hazards is to identify them. This can include anything from fear and anxiety to overconfidence and impulsivity. Once you have identified the hazards, the next step is to assess them. You need to understand how each hazard can impact your trading performance and what measures you can take to mitigate those risks.

Monitoring and reviewing your control measures is a critical step in psychological risk management. It's important to assess regularly whether your control measures are effective and adjust them as necessary. This is a continuous process, and you need to be vigilant in monitoring your psychological risks to ensure that they don't impact your trading.

Developing control measures is the final step in psychological risk management. This can include anything from mindfulness techniques to developing a trading plan. By having control measures in place, you can better manage your psychological risks and make informed trading decisions that align with your trading goals.

In summary, psychological risk management is an essential part of trading psychology. By identifying, assessing, monitoring, and developing control measures for psychological hazards, you can better manage your emotions and achieve financial success. Remember, managing psychological risks is a continuous process, and it requires discipline, strategy, and mental toughness to succeed.

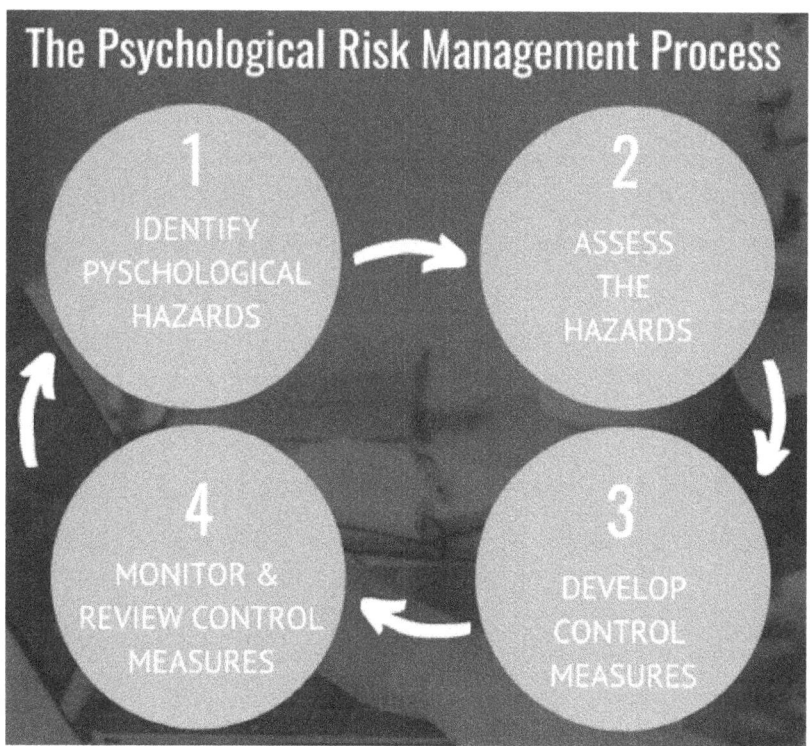

Overcoming Fear and Greed in Trading

Fear and greed are two of the most prevalent emotions that traders encounter. They have the potential to push us towards taking unwarranted risks or retaining losing trades for an extended period. This chapter delves into the influence of fear and greed on trading psychology and offers you techniques to conquer them.

While fear and greed are natural human emotions, they can be problematic when it comes to trading. Fear can cause traders to hesitate and miss profitable opportunities, while greed can lead to excessive risk-taking and poor decision-making. Therefore, it is essential to learn how to overcome these emotions and manage them effectively.

One approach to overcoming fear and greed is to develop a trading plan that outlines clear entry and exit points, risk management strategies, and profit targets. By having a plan in place, traders can reduce the impact of emotions on their decision-making and focus on following a set of predefined rules.

Another approach is to use mindfulness techniques to manage emotions. Mindfulness involves paying attention to the present moment without judgment and can help traders become more aware of their thoughts and emotions. By acknowledging and accepting their emotions, traders can make more rational decisions and avoid being driven solely by fear or greed.

It's important to remember that overcoming fear and greed is an ongoing process that requires practice and self-awareness. Traders may benefit from working with a trading coach or therapist to develop effective coping strategies and improve their emotional regulation skills.

Ultimately, by learning how to manage fear and greed, traders can make more rational and informed decisions, leading to greater trading success and financial gains.

Developing a Positive Mindset for Trading Success

Your mindset can have a powerful impact on your trading performance. A positive mindset can help you stay focused, confident, and resilient in the face of challenges, while a negative mindset can lead to self-doubt, fear, and missed opportunities. In this chapter, we will explore the importance of developing a positive mindset for trading success and provide you with practical strategies to do so.

One of the initial steps to develop a positive mindset is to shift your focus from the outcome to the process. Instead of obsessing over making a specific amount of money, concentrate on adhering to your trading plan and making wise trading choices. By concentrating on the process, you can evade the emotional ups and downs that come with frequently checking your account balance and instead remain focused on your trading objectives.

Another key strategy for developing a positive mindset is to practice gratitude. Take time each day to reflect on the things you are grateful for, both in your trading life and in your personal life. This can help shift your focus away from negative thoughts and feelings and help you maintain a positive outlook.

Additionally, learning to reframe negative thoughts and beliefs can be a powerful tool in developing a positive mindset. When faced with a setback or failure, try to reframe it as an opportunity for growth and learning. By reframing your negative thoughts, you can maintain a positive perspective and use challenges as a springboard for improvement.

Ultimately, developing a positive mindset is an ongoing process that requires practice and persistence. By adopting a positive mindset, you can better manage your emotions, stay focused on your trading goals, and achieve greater success in your trading endeavors.

The Role of Discipline in Trading Psychology

Discipline is a crucial aspect of successful trading, yet it is often one of the most challenging traits to develop. It requires a strong sense of self-control, the ability to stick to a plan, and the willingness to make difficult decisions even when emotions are running high.

In trading, discipline means having a set of rules and strategies that you follow consistently, even when the market is unpredictable or volatile. It means having the discipline to cut your losses when a trade isn't going your way, and to take profits when the time is right.

Developing discipline takes time and effort, but it is a critical component of trading psychology. It can help you stay focused, make rational decisions, and avoid the emotional pitfalls that can lead to costly mistakes.

One way to cultivate discipline is to develop a trading plan that outlines your goals, strategies, and risk management approach. Stick to your plan, even when the market is tempting you to deviate from it. Trust in your research and analysis, and have the discipline to stick to your strategy even when it's not immediately paying off.

Another way to develop discipline is to practice mindfulness and self-awareness. When you feel yourself getting caught up in emotions like fear, greed, or FOMO (fear of missing out), take a step back and assess the situation objectively. Take a deep breath, refocus your mind, and remind yourself of your trading plan and goals.

Remember, discipline is not about being perfect or never making mistakes. It's about having the courage and strength to stick to your plan and make the tough decisions that will ultimately lead to success.

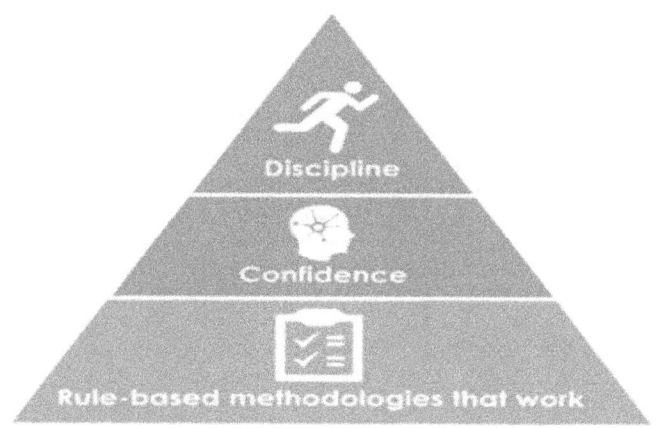

Strategies for Dealing with Trading Losses

One of the most challenging aspects of trading psychology is learning how to deal with losses. Losses are an inevitable part of trading, but they can be emotionally devastating if not managed properly. It's essential to have strategies in place for dealing with losses to prevent them from derailing your trading success.

One strategy for dealing with trading losses is to focus on the long-term. It's important to remember that no single trade or even a string of losses can define your overall trading success. Keep your eye on the bigger picture, and remember that losses are just a part of the journey.

Another strategy is to practice self-compassion. It's easy to be hard on yourself when you experience losses, but this can be counterproductive. Instead, try to be kind and understanding with yourself. Remember that losses are a natural part of the learning process, and that every trader experiences them.

One powerful strategy for dealing with losses is to use them as an opportunity to learn and grow. Analyze your losses and try to identify what went wrong. Use this information to refine your strategies and improve your decision-making in the future.

Trading and Emotional Intelligence

As a trader, you've probably experienced the intense emotions that can arise during a trade. Fear, greed, frustration - these emotions can be overwhelming and can even lead to poor decision making. But what if you could harness the power of your emotions to become a more successful trader? That's where emotional intelligence comes in.

Emotional intelligence is the capacity to identify and handle your own emotions, along with those of others. Emotional intelligence can be the crucial factor in unleashing your complete potential as a trader when it comes to trading.

Imagine being able to identify the emotions that arise during a trade and manage them effectively. You'd be able to make decisions based on logic and reason, rather than being driven by fear or greed. By developing your emotional intelligence, you can do just that.

One powerful strategy for developing emotional intelligence in trading is mindfulness. By practicing mindfulness, you can become more attuned to your thoughts and emotions, allowing you to manage them more effectively. You'll be able to stay focused and present in the moment, rather than getting caught up in emotions that could cloud your judgement.

Another important aspect of emotional intelligence in trading is empathy. Empathy involves being able to understand and relate to the emotions of others

Emotional Intelligence = Less Shame

Overcoming Trading Addiction

Trading addiction is a serious problem that can have devastating consequences. It can lead to financial ruin, strained relationships, and even physical and mental health issues. But how do you know if you're addicted to trading? And more importantly, how do you overcome it?

First and foremost, it's important to recognize the signs of trading addiction. Do you feel a constant urge to trade, even when it's not financially responsible? Do you neglect other important aspects of your life, like relationships or work, in favor of trading? Do you feel a sense of euphoria or excitement while trading, even if you're not making a profit?

If you answered yes to any of these questions, you may be struggling with trading addiction. But don't worry, there are steps you can take to overcome it.

One of the most effective ways to overcome trading addiction is to seek professional help. This may involve working with a therapist or counsellor who specializes in addiction treatment. They can help you identify the root causes of your addiction and develop strategies for managing it.

Another important step is to establish healthy habits and routines. This may involve setting limits on your trading activity, taking breaks, and focusing on other areas of your life that bring you joy and fulfillment.

Finally, it's important to surround yourself with a supportive community. This may involve joining a trading support group or connecting with other traders who are also working to overcome addiction. By building a support system, you'll have the encouragement and accountability you need to stay on track.

Remember, trading addiction is a serious issue, but it's not insurmountable. With the right tools and support, you can overcome it and achieve a healthy, fulfilling life both in and out of the trading world.

Developing Resilience in Trading

As a trader, you will inevitably face setbacks and losses. It's how you respond to those setbacks that ultimately determines your success. Developing resilience is crucial for overcoming these challenges and staying in the game.

Resilience isn't something that comes naturally to everyone. It's a skill that can be developed with practice and dedication. In this chapter, we'll explore the mindset and habits of resilient traders and provide practical strategies for developing your own resilience.

We'll start by looking at the characteristics of resilient traders. Resilient traders have a growth mindset, meaning they view challenges as opportunities for growth and learning. They are able to regulate their emotions and maintain a positive attitude even in the face of adversity. They have strong problem-solving skills and are able to adapt to changing market conditions.

So, how can you develop these characteristics and become a more resilient trader? One key strategy is to focus on the things you can control. While you can't control market movements or the actions of other traders, you can control your own behavior and mindset. By focusing on the things you can control, you'll feel more empowered and less helpless when things don't go as planned.

Another important strategy is to cultivate a strong support system. This can include other traders, mentors, friends, and family members who understand and support your trading journey. Having people in your corner who can offer encouragement, advice, and perspective can help you stay motivated and resilient when things get tough.

We'll also explore the role of self-care in developing resilience. Taking care of your physical, mental, and emotional health is essential for staying resilient and avoiding burnout. This can include regular exercise, healthy eating habits, meditation or mindfulness practices, and prioritizing rest and relaxation.

Remember, resilience is not something that happens overnight. It's a process that requires time, effort, and dedication. By developing your resilience, you'll be better equipped to handle the ups and downs of trading and ultimately achieve long-term success.

Managing Trading Stress

Trading can be a highly stressful endeavor. The pressure of making quick decisions and the potential financial losses can create intense stress that can negatively impact a trader's performance. In this chapter, we will explore the different types of trading stress and provide strategies to help manage them.

First, it's important to recognize the different types of stress that traders can experience. There's the stress of uncertainty, which comes from the unknowns of the market and the potential for unexpected events to occur. Then there's the stress of losses, which can lead to feelings of anxiety, frustration, and self-doubt. Finally, there's the stress of performance, where traders may feel pressure to perform at a certain level and meet their financial goals.

One effective strategy for managing trading stress is to practice mindfulness. Mindfulness involves being present in the moment and fully aware of your thoughts and feelings without judgment. By being mindful, traders can better regulate their emotions and make more rational trading decisions. Techniques like meditation, deep breathing exercises, and visualization can also help to reduce stress and increase focus.

Another strategy is to engage in physical activity. Exercise is a great way to release tension and reduce stress levels. Whether it's a brisk walk, yoga, or weightlifting, physical activity can help traders to clear their minds and refocus their energy.

Finally, it's important to have a support system in place. Trading can be a lonely profession, and having a network of friends, family, or fellow traders to talk to can help to reduce feelings of isolation and stress. Online trading communities can also be a valuable resource for traders to connect with others and gain support.

Managing trading stress is crucial for success in the markets. By recognizing the different types of stress, practicing mindfulness, engaging in physical activity, and building a support system, traders can better manage their emotions and make more informed trading decisions.

Dealing with Trading Regrets and Mistakes

Trading is a field that is filled with high risks and uncertainties. Every trader has made mistakes or had trades that didn't go as planned. These losses can leave you with feelings of regret and disappointment, making it difficult to move on and learn from the experience. In this chapter, we will discuss the importance of dealing with trading regrets and mistakes and how to overcome them.

Regrets and mistakes can be a powerful teacher, but only if you're willing to learn from them. One of the first steps in dealing with trading regrets is to accept that they happen to everyone. Even the most experienced traders have made mistakes and had trades that didn't go as planned. By acknowledging that these experiences are a natural part of the trading journey, you can begin to move past them and focus on the future.

Another important aspect of dealing with trading regrets is to examine the reasons why the trade didn't go as planned. This can involve reviewing your trading plan, analyzing market conditions, and identifying any cognitive biases that may have influenced your decision-making. By understanding the factors that led to the loss, you can learn from the experience and improve your trading strategy.

In addition to examining the reasons for the loss, it's also important to practice self-compassion. Be kind to yourself and acknowledge that trading is a challenging and emotional endeavor. It's okay to make mistakes, and you can use them as an opportunity for growth and learning.

Finally, it's important to create a plan for moving forward. This can involve making changes to your trading strategy, seeking out mentorship or education, or simply taking a break from trading to regroup. By having a plan in place, you can move past your regrets and mistakes and continue on your trading journey with renewed focus and determination.

Remember, trading regrets and mistakes are a natural part of the trading journey. By learning from them and developing resilience, you can become a better trader and achieve your financial goals.

The Psychology of Successful Trading

Successful trading is not just about having a solid trading plan and executing it flawlessly. It also requires the right mindset and a deep understanding of your own psychological tendencies. In this chapter, we will explore the psychology of successful trading and what separates the most successful traders from the rest.

First and foremost, successful traders have a deep understanding of themselves. They know their strengths and weaknesses and how these can impact their trading decisions. They are also aware of their emotions and know how to manage them effectively. By understanding themselves, successful traders are able to make better decisions and avoid common trading mistakes.

Another key trait of successful traders is discipline. They have a set of rules that they follow consistently, regardless of market conditions. This allows them to avoid impulsive decisions and stick to their trading plan. Successful traders are also patient and understand that success in trading is a long-term game. They do not let short-term setbacks deter them from their goals.

Successful traders also have a growth mindset. They view losses as opportunities to learn and improve, rather than failures. They are constantly seeking to improve their trading strategies and techniques and are not afraid to try new things. They also understand that there is always more to learn and are open to feedback and constructive criticism.

Another important trait of successful traders is adaptability. They are able to adjust their trading strategies to changing market conditions, and are not afraid to make changes when necessary. Successful traders also understand the importance of risk management and always have a plan in place to limit potential losses.

Lastly, successful traders have a strong sense of confidence in their abilities. They understand that trading can be a difficult and unpredictable endeavor, but they also have the conviction that they can succeed. This confidence allows them to stay focused and disciplined, even in the face of adversity.

In conclusion, the psychology of successful trading is complex and multifaceted. It requires a deep understanding of oneself, discipline, patience, a growth mindset, adaptability, risk management, and confidence. By developing these traits and incorporating them into your trading strategy, you too can become a successful trader.

Bringing it All Together: Integrating Trading Psychology into Your Trading Strategy

Congratulations! You have learned a great deal about trading psychology and how it can impact your trading success. Now, it's time to bring it all together and integrate your newfound knowledge into your trading strategy.

First and foremost, it's important to remember that trading psychology is not a one-size-fits-all approach. What works for one trader may not work for another, so it's crucial to find a strategy that works best for you.

One effective way to integrate trading psychology into your trading strategy is to develop a trading plan that incorporates your psychological strengths and weaknesses. For example, if you know that you struggle with impulsivity, your trading plan should include strategies to help you avoid making impulsive trades. Alternatively, if you tend to struggle with fear and hesitation, your plan should include techniques to help you overcome those emotions and make confident trades.

It's important to remember that your trading plan should be flexible and adaptable. As you grow and evolve as a trader, your psychological strengths and weaknesses may change, and your plan should reflect that. Don't be afraid to make adjustments and tweak your plan as needed to better suit your current situation.

Another way to integrate trading psychology into your trading strategy is to use your emotions as a tool. Rather than letting your emotions control you, use them to your advantage. For example, if you feel anxious or fearful about a trade, take a step back and assess the situation. Is there a valid reason for your fear, or is it simply an emotional response? Use your fear as a signal to examine the trade more closely and make an informed decision.

Finally, always remember to take care of your mental and emotional health. Trading can be a stressful and demanding profession, and it's important to take time to decompress and recharge. Whether it's through exercise, meditation, or simply spending time with loved ones, make sure you are prioritizing your mental and emotional wellbeing.

In conclusion, trading psychology is a crucial component of trading success. By integrating your psychological strengths and weaknesses into your trading plan, using your emotions as a tool, and prioritizing your mental and emotional health, you can become a more effective and profitable trader. Good luck on your trading journey!

"THE GOAL OF A SUCCESSFUL TRADER IS TO MAKE BEST TRADE POSSIBLE MONEY IS SECONDARY"

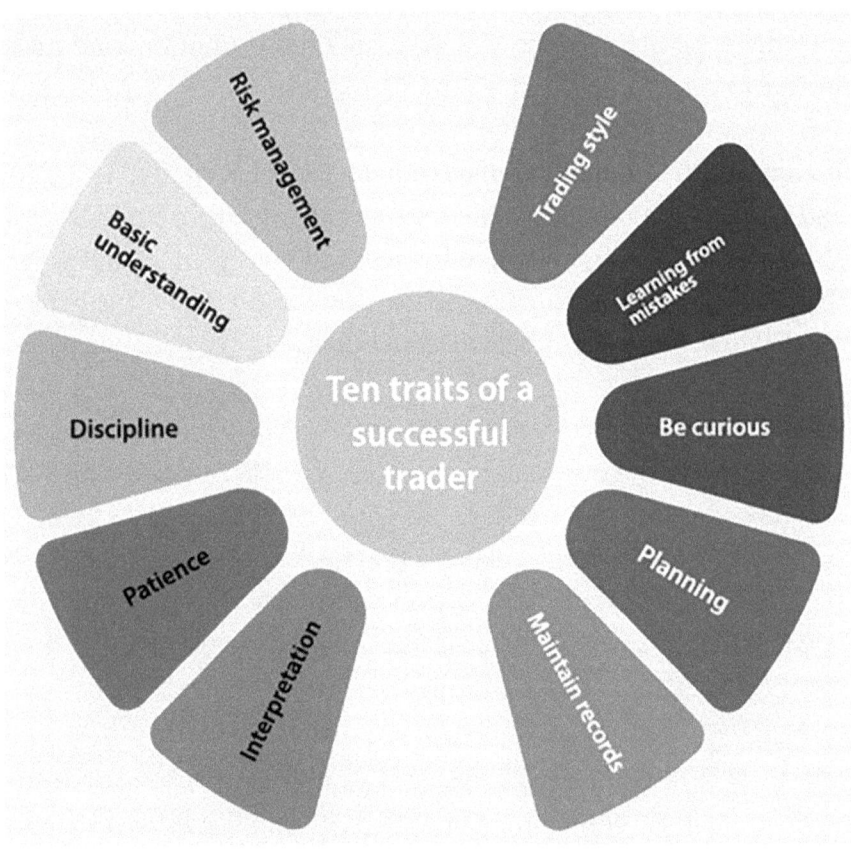

CHAPTER 16

DAILY AFFIRMATION FOR TRADERS FOR A STRONG MINDSET

Daily affirmations hold a significant importance in our lives as they have the power to shape our thoughts, beliefs, and actions.

These simple statements, when practiced with belief and intention, have the ability to shape your reality and guide you towards a more empowered and fulfilling existence.

Imagine this: Each morning, as the sun rises, you take a moment to close your eyes and say positive things to yourself. You might say, "I am confident, capable, and deserving of success." With every repetition, these words sink deep into your being, rewiring your thoughts, beliefs, and actions.

The magic lies in your mind. As you affirm your worth, your mind becomes fertile ground for self-confidence and self-belief to grow. No longer held back by doubt or fear, you walk through life with certainty, knowing that you deserve all the great things that come your way.

But daily affirmations are not just about wishful thinking. They inspire you to take action. When you affirm your strengths, resilience, and abilities, you become unstoppable. You face challenges head-on, seeing them as opportunities for growth.

Through daily affirmations, you infuse your thoughts with positivity, banishing self-limiting beliefs. You rewrite the stories you tell yourself, replacing doubt and fear with courage, abundance, and possibility.

However, remember that daily affirmations require consistency and a connection to your inner self. They ask you to confront fears, let go of old identities, and embrace who you truly are.

As you embark on this transformative journey, remember that affirmations are not just words. They are the brushstrokes of your life's masterpiece. Embrace them with passion and conviction, and witness your life transform into a vibrant canvas filled with joy, success, and limitless potential.

Use the following affirmation before opening the market every morning and repeat it a minimum of three times on your trading station.

1. I am an exceptional day trader.
2. I approach the markets with enthusiasm and focus.
3. I am patient and disciplined in my trading.
4. I make small losses and big profits.
5. Every trade offers an opportunity to learn and grow.
6. I am in control of my emotions during trading.
7. I have a solid trading plan and full confidence in it.
8. I am always seeking to improve my skills and knowledge.
9. I trust in the market's abundance of opportunities.
10. I am a successful and prosperous day trader.

CHAPTER 17

HOW TO CONTROL OVERTRADING

Overtrading is a common mistake that many traders make, which can lead to significant losses. If you find yourself taking too many trades or risking more than you should, it may be time to work on overcoming your overtrading habits. Here are some tips to help you get started:

1. Set clear trading goals: Before you start trading, it's important to have a clear idea of what you want to achieve. Set realistic trading goals and stick to them. This will help you focus on quality trades and avoid overtrading.
2. Use a trading plan: A trading plan is essential for any trader. It helps you stay disciplined and avoid impulsive trades. Your plan should include entry and exit points, stop loss levels, and risk management strategies.
3. Keep a trading journal: Keeping a trading journal can help you identify patterns in your trading behavior. Record your trades, including your thoughts and emotions at the time of the trade. This will help you identify when you are more likely to overtrade and why.
4. Take breaks: Overtrading can often be a result of trading for too long without taking a break. It's important to take regular breaks to clear your mind and refocus. Take a walk, read a book or do something else you enjoy to help you relax.
5. Learn to say no: Sometimes the best trade is no trade at all. Learning to say no to trades that don't meet your criteria can be challenging but is essential to avoid overtrading.

6. Control your emotions: Emotions can be a significant factor in overtrading. Fear, greed, and FOMO (fear of missing out) can lead to impulsive trades. Take the time to recognize and control your emotions when trading.
7. Use risk management: Risk management is crucial for avoiding overtrading. Use stop-loss orders to limit your losses, and don't risk more than you can afford to lose. Stick to your risk management plan, and don't deviate from it.

By following these tips, you can start to overcome your overtrading habits and become a more disciplined and profitable trader. Remember, trading is a marathon, not a sprint. Focus on quality trades and avoid overtrading to achieve long-term success.

CHAPTER 18

TWT 3-3-4 CONCEPT

Have you ever wondered why some people seem to excel in every area of their lives while others struggle to make progress? The answer lies in the concept of 334, which has the power to transform every aspect of your life - both personal and professional.

So, what is the 334 concept? It's a simple yet powerful framework that consists of three parts. The first "3" represents the fact that we can only retain 30% of the information we learn, whether from reading a book or watching a video.

Shocking, isn't it? But the good news is that the next 30% comes from putting that learning into action. Knowledge is only potential power, but taking action on that knowledge is where the real power lies. This brings the total to 60%, but how can we achieve the remaining 40%?

The final 40% comes from having a mentor or coach who can guide us through our ups and downs, correct us when we're wrong, and help us master the concept in the most effective way. They can help us understand the material in a way that suits our learning style and motivate us when we're feeling discouraged.

Remember, finding a mentor is key to mastering any concept, including trading. While you may have learned the basics from a book or video, a mentor can help you adapt that knowledge to your individual situation and correct any mistakes you may make along the way.

If you're serious about becoming a successful and profitable trader, finding the right coach can help you reach that destination much faster than you ever imagined. So, what are you waiting for? Go out and find yourself a mentor who can help you master your craft and transform your life!

CHAPTER 19
SECRET SAUCE TO BECOME AN INDEPENDENT TRADER

"GOALS ARE FOR LOSERS BECAUSE WINNERS HAVE SYSTEM"

Trading System

A trading system is your ultimate weapon, your secret recipe for success in this thrilling adventure.

Think of it as your personal trading guru, guiding you through the maze of financial markets. With its arsenal of rules and strategies, it becomes your trusted ally, helping you navigate the turbulent waters of buying and selling.

Picture yourself analysing complex charts, deciphering mysterious patterns, and spotting hidden signals that others might miss. It's like uncovering the hidden treasure map that leads to untold riches.

But trading is not just about luck or gut feelings. Oh no! A solid trading system is built on a foundation of careful research, combining the art of technical analysis with the science of fundamental analysis. It's a symphony of numbers, news, and market psychology, all intertwined to reveal the perfect trade.

With your trading system as your faithful companion, you can stay one step ahead of the crowd. It tells you when to pounce on a golden opportunity and when to retreat to protect your hard-earned profits.

It's a game of strategy and risk management, where your moves are calculated and precise.

Building a trading system requires careful planning and consideration. Here are some steps to help you get started:

1. Define your trading goals: Determine what you want to achieve through trading. Are you looking for short-term profits or long-term investments? Clarify your financial goals and risk tolerance.
2. Choose your trading style: Select a trading style that suits your personality and preferences. Options include day trading, swing trading, or position trading. Each style has different timeframes and strategies.
3. Conduct thorough research: Dive deep into the financial markets you wish to trade. Study the instruments, such as stocks, currencies, or commodities, and understand their dynamics. Stay updated with relevant news, economic indicators, and market trends.
4. Develop a strategy: Based on your research, create a trading strategy that outlines your entry and exit points. Determine which indicators or patterns you will use to identify opportunities. Consider factors like risk management, position sizing, and profit targets.
5. Test your strategy: Back test your trading strategy using historical data to see how it would have performed in the past. This step helps you evaluate its effectiveness and make any necessary adjustments.
6. Set clear rules: Define specific rules for entering and exiting trades. These rules should be based on your strategy and account for various scenarios, including market volatility and unexpected events.
7. Implement risk management: Establish risk management techniques to protect your capital. Determine your maximum risk per trade and set stop-loss orders to limit potential losses. Additionally, consider diversifying your portfolio to spread risk.

8. Monitor and adjust: Regularly monitor your trades and review their performance. Keep a trading journal to record your observations and learn from your experiences. Adjust your strategy as needed, taking into account changing market conditions.
9. Continuously educate yourself: Stay updated with market developments, new trading techniques, and evolving strategies. Attend seminars, read books, and follow reputable financial publications to enhance your trading knowledge.
10. Practice discipline and patience: Stick to your trading system and avoid impulsive decisions based on emotions. Maintain discipline, even during losing streaks, and remember that consistency is key to long-term success.

Are you tired of hearing about the principles of building a trading system without anyone showing you how to do it? Well, worry no more! Trading with Tarun is here to unveil the practical secrets and guide you through the exhilarating process.

Get ready for the four easy TWT steps that will empower you to create your very own trading system:

Step 1: Embrace Risk Management like a Pro!

Say goodbye to reckless gambling and hello to a well-defined risk management plan. Determine the amount you're willing to lose and the capital you're ready to risk. Personally, I follow a minimum 1:2 risk and reward ratio or even better! I never, ever risk more than 30% of my total income on a single trade. Let's protect that hard-earned money!

Step 2: Craft Your Winning Strategy!

Discover the strategy that resonates with your trading style and consistently delivers desired results. Whether it's based on price action or indicators, find the one that sets your trading soul on fire.

And guess what? We'll reveal the best way to find that strategy in our next step. Get ready for success!

Step 3: Unleash the Power of Trade Journaling!

Unlock the secrets hidden within your trades by journaling every single one of them. Explore which time frames work best for you, identify the strategies that rake in the maximum profits, and learn from your successes and failures. The path to greatness lies in analysing and adapting. Let's uncover your unique trading edge!

Step 4: Combine, Create, and Conquer!

It's time to bring it all together. Combine your risk management plan, your winning strategy, and the insights from your trade journaling. Wrap them in a cocoon of discipline and commitment. Follow your rules with unwavering dedication, and witness the magic unfold. Prepare to maximize your trading potential and achieve remarkable results.

Trading with Tarun is your gateway to practical guidance and real-world trading success. No more vague theories or empty promises. It's time to take action, seize control, and build your own trading empire. Let's embark on this thrilling journey together!

CHAPTER

20 TRADING JOURNAL SAMPLE

CHAPTER 21

MY TRADING JOURNEY

As I reflect on my journey in the stock market, I can't help but feel a mix of emotions. There were moments of excitement, greed, fear, frustration, and eventually, redemption.

Once, someone very wise said, "It's not the destination, but the journey we should enjoy making it memorable." These words hold true in my life as I embarked on a journey that changed my career path from a corporate training professional to a full-time trader.

I spent eight wonderful years in Dubai, working and exploring new cultures, meeting people, and traveling the world. One Friday evening, I was spending time with my dear friend Arjit, who has been my support system in Dubai. We were playing a game of FIFA on PS4, and he was winning, as usual. However, my interest started to wane, as I kept losing game after game.

Arjit noticed my disinterest and suggested we try a new game. Suddenly, his phone beeped, and he received a message. He looked ecstatic after reading it, so I asked him what had happened. He shared that he had received a dividend from one of the stocks he had purchased. I didn't know what to say, so I congratulated him, hoping to end the conversation.

However, he persisted, saying that we could trade stocks together and make a fortune. He said that the stock market had huge potential, and we could change our lives if we entered the market. I declined, saying that I didn't understand the stock market, didn't like it, and had no interest in it.

Arjit then said something that struck a chord within me. He said that everything in life is tough, complicated, and uncomfortable until we learn how to do it or give it a try. He challenged me to learn about the stock market and promised that it would be easy once I started.

His words resonated with me, and I agreed to give it a shot. I asked him what to do next, and he suggested opening a Demat account and adding funds to start trading. And so, my journey as a full-time trader began, and I never looked back.

In just a couple of days, I opened a Demat account with Sherkhan and deposited 2 lakh rupees for trading. Initially, my equity trading strategy didn't yield much profit. However, one day, the RM of Sherkhan introduced me to option trading. He claimed that by activating my F&O services, I could earn a daily profit of 50%. Although it sounded too good to be true, as an Indian, I was a dreamer and loved quick results. Therefore, I activated the service without hesitation.

I still remember the exhilaration I felt when I made 25,000 Rupees with just a 1 lac investment on my first trade! That was a 25% return in just 30 minutes! My mind began racing with thoughts of buying bungalows, big cars, and anything else my heart desired. But, as you might expect, my beginner's luck didn't last long.

In just 10 days, I had lost 2 lakh rupees along with the profits I had earned. I was in debt for a total of 2 lakhs and was unsure of how to inform my friend about it. Eventually, I gathered the courage to confess, and he simply smiled and said, "Bhai, loss sabka hota hai. Don't worry." He suggested that I educate myself more about the market and invest more funds.

Determined to turn things around, I added 1 lakh more to my account and tried to be more disciplined and wise with my trades. But as they say, **"EK baar Bank Nifty ka shauk chadhe to Kahe ka Discipline or kahe ka risk management."** In just seven days, that additional 1 lakh was gone, and I was in a total loss of 3 lakhs.

I was furious and frustrated with myself, but at least I had the consolation of knowing that the money was mine and not borrowed from someone else. I found solace in the fact that no one was coming after me to pay it back. Unfortunately, many others who take loans or borrow money from others are not as fortunate and often realize their mistakes too late.

So, I took a break from trading and focused on my job for a few days. However, one day, I received a message from someone claiming to be a professional Stock Market support provider. They promised to help me recover my losses with lightning speed.

Initially, I thought it was a good idea to seek assistance from a professional and take a risk. Perhaps my lost funds would be recovered, and if their claims were accurate, I would regain profitability in a brief period.

As you might have guessed, these were the same Telegram and WhatsApp service providers who give tips and advice to people, claiming to help them make money.

So, I added two more lakh rupees and started working on the tips provided by the provider. He asked me to buy Bank Nifty Call options, and the market started to fall.

I messaged him and asked for a stop loss, but he said, "Don't worry, hold." The market went further down, and I messaged him again, but he gave me the same response.

Then, the market went even lower, and he asked me to average down and hold it for the next day. I was scared, but I did as he said. The next day, there was a big gap down of 700+ points. I messaged him, but he didn't reply. I even called him, but he didn't answer.

That day, I wrote a motivational quote for myself and traders like me, which was:

> **"TIPS ARE FOR WAITERS IN RESTAURANTS, NOT FOR TRADERS IN THE STOCK MARKET."**
> **- Tarun Sharma**

Within two days, I lost another two lakh rupees, and my total loss was over five lakh rupees. That day, after my meditation session, I realized that trading is a zero-sum game. If someone is losing, someone else is making money. I needed to learn that way before I started trading again because I refused to be a loser in this game.

I started learning from books, YouTube, and workshops to make my own strategies. It took me three months to restart trading, and in just two months, I recovered my five lakh rupees and became a profitable trader.

Now, I'm doing it all by myself, but I'm still learning every day to enhance my skillset and knowledge. Remember, there is no earning without learning, hence "learn before you earn."

Unleashing the Trader Within: A Journey of Unexpected Inspiration

It was a tranquil evening when I found myself attending an open session conducted by my dear friend Sakshi, an accomplished L&D professional whom I had met during my time in Dubai. Sakshi hosted a seminar called "Candid Conversation - With Sakshi," where individuals with shared interests engaged in thought-provoking discussions.

During one such gathering, the topic of discussion centred around the importance of mastering a subject before offering advice or suggestions to others in that particular field. As the conversation unfolded, Sakshi posed a question that resonated deeply within me: **"Recall a time when you confidently advised someone on a topic you had no prior experience in."**

The question lingered in the air, urging me to reflect on my own experiences. It was then that I realized, for the better part of four to five years, I had been persistently encouraging my former boss, Dharam, to write a book. Dharam possessed a wealth of knowledge in the realm of L&D that had the potential to benefit countless individuals if only he would pen it down and share it with the world.

Every time I broached the subject with Dharam, he would respond with a warm smile, assuring me, "Yes, my friend, I will do it soon." Yet, that "soon" never arrived. Still, undeterred by his delay, I continued to implore him to undertake the task. The irony was not lost on me—I had no experience in writing a book, and to make matters worse, I was not particularly fond of reading. My preferred methods of learning revolved around audio and visual mediums, as I considered myself an auditory and visual learner.

However, the realization struck me like a bolt of lightning. How could I continue to urge someone else to embark on a task I had never attempted myself? It was at this crossroad of self-reflection that I made a resolute decision—to write this book.

And so, armed with determination and an unwavering belief in the power of experience, I embarked on an unexpected journey. Little did I know that this decision would set into motion a series of events that would shape my life in unimaginable ways.

Writing a book was a daunting task, especially for someone like me who had never immersed themselves in the world of literature. However, I chose to view this unfamiliar territory as an opportunity for growth, an invitation to explore uncharted waters.

With each passing day, my excitement grew as I delved deeper into the craft of storytelling. I discovered the power of words, how they could evoke emotions, transport readers to distant lands, and ignite the spark of inspiration within their hearts. It was an exhilarating experience to witness my ideas take shape, transforming into a narrative that could captivate and empower readers.

The journey from the inception of the book to its publication was not without its challenges. Doubts crept in, whispering tales of inadequacy and questioning my ability to bring this project to fruition. However, the unwavering support of those around me, including friends, students, and even strangers who had heard whispers of my endeavor, pushed me forward.

With each passing day, the manuscript grew, taking shape and form like a masterpiece in progress. The words danced across the pages, weaving a tapestry of knowledge, experiences, and insights. But the true test awaited me: transforming this labor of love into a tangible creation that could reach the hands and minds of readers.

I sought guidance from seasoned authors and publishing professionals, eagerly absorbing their wisdom like a sponge. The publishing process, with its intricacies and intricacies, unfolded before me. From editing and proofreading to cover design and formatting, every step brought me closer to my dream becoming a reality.

Finally, the day arrived when "Unleash the Trader Within" was ready to make its debut in the world. As the book hit the shelves and online platforms, a wave of gratitude washed over me. I was immensely thankful to Sakshi, Dharam, Arjit, Varaang, Shikha, Divya and all the individuals who had played a part in making this book come to life.

CHAPTER 22

LETTER TO THE DAY TRADER FROM THE AUTHOR

Dear Champ,

As a day trader, you are a warrior of the markets, a brave soul who faces each day with courage and determination. You are an artist of the trade, a master of the charts, and a wizard of numbers. You are the embodiment of success, the epitome of dedication, and the personification of discipline.

You know that success is not given, it is earned. You understand that it takes hard work, perseverance, and a relentless pursuit of knowledge to achieve greatness in the markets. And you are willing to put in the time and effort to make your dreams a reality.

You embrace the challenges that come your way, knowing that they are opportunities to learn and grow. You see each trade as a chance to prove yourself, to push yourself to new heights, and to achieve more than you ever thought possible.

You are confident in your abilities, knowing that you have the skills, knowledge, and discipline to succeed. You trust in yourself and your strategies, and you know that you have what it takes to overcome any obstacle that may come your way.

You are driven by your passion for the markets, your love of the game, and your desire to achieve financial freedom. You understand that the markets are not just a means to an end, but a way of life, a path to a better future.

And above all, you believe in yourself. You know that you have what it takes to succeed, and you are willing to do whatever it takes to make your dreams a reality. You are a day trader, a warrior of the markets, and a true champion of success.

> "Let the stock market be the fuel that ignites your dreams, propelling you towards a future where aspirations become achievements."
> - Tarun Sharma

CHAPTER 23
DISCLAIMER FOR READERS

The information and strategies presented in this book on technical analysis and price action are intended for educational purposes only. They are based on my personal experiences and observations in the stock market.

I am not a licensed financial advisor, and the content provided in this book should not be considered as financial advice or a recommendation to buy or sell any securities. The strategies discussed may not be suitable for every individual or market condition.

It is important to understand that trading and investing in the stock market involve inherent risks, and there is no guarantee of profit. The performance of any investment or trading strategy can vary and may result in both gains and losses.

I, Tarun, and my company, Trading with Tarun, cannot be held responsible for any direct or indirect losses, financial or otherwise, that may occur because of applying the concepts, strategies, or information provided in this book. The readers and users of this book are solely responsible for their own investment decisions and actions.

Before implementing any strategies discussed in this book, it is strongly recommended that readers engage in paper trading for a minimum period of 21 days. Paper trading refers to the simulated trading of securities without actual financial risk. By practicing the strategies in a paper trading environment, readers can gain experience and assess the effectiveness of the strategies without risking real money.

The purpose of the 21-day paper trading period is to allow readers to familiarize themselves with the strategies, understand their strengths and limitations, and evaluate their compatibility with personal trading styles and risk tolerance. It provides an opportunity to refine the techniques and build confidence before considering live trading.

By reading this book, you acknowledge and agree that you will engage in the recommended 21-day paper trading period, as advised by Tarun, before making any decisions to apply the strategies discussed in a real trading account. You understand that this period is essential for gaining experience, testing the strategies, and making informed choices.

You also acknowledge that trading and investing in the stock market still carry risks, even after the paper trading period. Therefore, it is crucial to exercise caution and continue monitoring the performance of the strategies in a real trading account. You agree to release and hold harmless Tarun, Trading with Tarun, and any associated individuals from any liability for losses, damages, or expenses incurred because of your actions in the stock market.

SO, WHAT'S NEXT?

Congratulations! You have just unlocked the secrets of the language of candlestick patterns, chart patterns, and the Trading with Tarun 5-star Day Trading setup. This knowledge is more powerful than you can imagine, and it has the potential to transform your trading style and make you an independent trader in no time.

But here's the thing - just having this knowledge is not enough. You need to put it into action and apply it to the charts. It's like having a genie in a lamp - you have the power, but you need to make the effort to unleash it. In trading, that effort comes in the form of practice and mastering your craft. There are no shortcuts to success, but with dedication and hard work, you can achieve your financial goals.

And that's not all! We have included bonus content to further enhance your trading journey. Keep practicing, stay motivated, and success will be within your reach.

DO YOU WANT MORE STUFF LIKE THIS?

Apple Store

Android Store

www.ingramcontent.com/pod-product-compliance
Lightning Source LLC
Chambersburg PA
CBHW040107180526
45172CB00009B/1261